Praise for *Love Work:*

Love Work:
Skills for Staying in Love

Love Work:
Skills for Staying in Love

by
Walter H. Mehring III, Ed.S
Licensed Professional Counselor
Licensed Marriage and Family Therapist

Published by
Hungrytown Press
3893 Hungrytown Road
Covesville, Virginia 22931
www.relationshipsrepair.com

For Polly,
My Dearest Love,
who liked my smile,
and decided I was worth keeping.

Thank you, Katie Hoffman, for thoughtful editing, kind testimonial and encouragement to publish.

Thank you, Jonathan Mehring, for your cover photo that so beautifully captures the idea of a relationship as a journey together, and for your portrait and copy editing. Thank you especially for your help and support in getting Love Work published.

Thank you, Heather Waraksa, for your design and layout expertise.

Table of Contents

Preface

I grew up in a family that was typical of small communities in Virginia in the 1950's. Only certain feelings were allowed. Everyone was supposed to be bright, good looking and happy. We emulated TV shows like "Ozzie and Harriet" and "Leave it to Beaver." Negative feelings were considered socially unacceptable and were to be avoided. We were to "put our best foot forward," "have a stiff upper lip," and "keep on the sunny side." Unfortunately, this emotional suppression led to painful family tensions and negative behavior patterns in spite of our best efforts to be the American ideal. These struggles led to my interest in relationships and my thirty years work counseling individuals, families, and couples.

Over time I have concluded that that these awkward, difficult-to-define-or-express things we call "feelings," rather than being threats that must be avoided or problems needing to be fixed, instead are the glue that holds our relationships together. Couples who learn to manage feelings in their relationships can leave exhaustion and struggle behind and, instead, find new energy and enjoyment in each other. I call the skill set to achieve this miracle *Love Work*.

Today, human difficulties with feelings are more acute than ever. Because so many people have developed their social skills indirectly through electronic media, partners often feel at a loss when they have to deal with issues in face to face intimate relationships. *Love Work* teaches couples how to live comfortably with each other in the real world. — Walter Mehring —

Why This Book?

I have found that couples have the following needs:

1) Couples need to feel safe and loved in their relationships.
2) Couples need common sense skills for taking care of their emotional needs.
3) Couples need help that promotes their reliance on themselves.
4) Couples have limited money, energy, and time, so they need help that is brief and offers immediate relief.

To meet these needs, I have developed *Love Work,* a short book that offers the reader a useful model for how relationships work and helps them develop skills with which they can build, repair, and maintain their relationships over a lifetime.

Modern couples face an ever-changing landscape of problems as life and technology rapidly change around them. As a result, couples frequently find themselves feeling unhappy, anxious, and that their relationships are stressed and under pressure. *Love Work* offers skills to help couples explore and respond to each partner's changing emotional needs in the present moment. This enables couples to understand each other and keep emotional pressure at a comfortable level. Through this process, couples can rediscover each other's emotional world, and feel calm and secure in their relationship.

While *Love Work* is offered in a self-help format for couples desiring comfortable long-term relationships with their partners, counselors from a wide variety of therapeutic orientations and job situations also will find the *Love Work* approach useful in helping their clients

deal successfully with many different kinds of human
relationships.

Chapter 1
What *Love Work* Offers

It feels so good when our interpersonal relationships are going well. And so bad when they aren't! We love to feel good and well connected to those we care about. Yet problems, once they start, often seem to take on a life of their own, leaving us feeling alone and abandoned in spite of all of our best efforts to get back on track.

Love Work will help you understand why these difficulties arise, what you can do to rebuild your connection, and how you can manage your love relationship's development over the long term. *Love Work* offers skills you and your partner can use to explore the emotional world of your relationship and make you both feel safe and cared for. With this emotional support, you will find yourselves able to put aside fruitless pain and struggle. Instead, you will be able to focus your energy outward, as a team, to deal confidently with whatever issues may confront you.

A unifying theme throughout this book is that these invisible awkward things we call "feelings," which frequently confront us in spite of our efforts to avoid them, are essential ingredients in smoothly functioning relationships. *Love Work* is a fitting title because the positive feelings we share with our partner create our sense of *love* in our relationship, and it takes a certain amount of *work* to maintain that connection. *Falling in love is easy. It takes some effort to stay there.*

This book will help you develop a clear understanding of your needs both as individuals and as a couple–and help you create effective strategies for getting those needs met. I use "he" and "she" for convenience to differentiate between partners, and "they" when referring to either partner. However, the roles described are interchangeable and the skills offered apply as well for LGBTQ couples.

Skill Mastery

Love Work helps you master four sets of skills:
1) Your Search Path shows you how to take care of your partner. Use this process when you are fine, but your partner is upset about something. You learn ways to calm your partner's emotions and gain a deeper understanding of your partner's emotional world.

2) Your Share Path shows you how to take care of yourself. Use this process when you yourself are upset about something, but your partner doesn't understand. You learn skills for standing up for yourself in ways that encourage your partner to give you the care you need.

3) Your Action Path teaches you how to get things done with your partner. Here you learn 6 ways to influence your partner's behavior in ways that allow you to deal with life's daily chores and challenges as a team. You will also learn to make conscious choices as to which approach is most likely to get your needs met with the least hassle.

4) Skill Integration teaches you strategies for using these skill sets together. This will enable you to maintain your caring cooperative relationship through the full gamut of life situations that will confront you.

You will find the basic concepts easy to understand. However, they can be difficult to use in real-life situations without practice. This is like learning to ride a bicycle. In your bike's case, what to do is easy to describe: "Simply get on and start pedaling. In order to keep your balance, turn the handle bars in whichever direction you are starting to fall." While this description is accurate, it still takes practice to get the hang of it.

The same is true in learning new relationship skills. Understanding the skills is only the first step. Practice is necessary to change how the neurons in your brain connect so that you can use the skills easily. To help you make these skills truly yours, you will be given situations through which you can practice the skills you have been reading about with your partner or interested friends. As you play the *Love Work* games, you turn ideas into skills you are comfortable using. This will enable you to use your new skills successfully in real life situations with your partner.

Love Work Assumptions

Love Work works well for many couples. It operates on the following assumptions:

• Both of you freely choose to be in your relationship.

- You would like to have an honest, relaxed, secure relationship with your partner.
- You are willing to have a mutually respectful relationship.
- You are willing to learn to deal with emotions, even intense negative ones, in your relationship.
- You are willing to learn to put your own emotional responses on hold for a time while you take care of your partner.

What Kinds of Problems Can *Love Work* Address?

Love Work looks at relationship problems as the result of unresolved emotional pressure existing *between* partners, rather than the litany of dissatisfactions and violations which couples often assume are the cause of their pain. Hence, when couples develop skills to reduce this pressure, rebuilding their connection and finding mutual understanding becomes much easier. Once couples are relaxed and working together, conflicts are more easily worked out or reduce in importance.

Relationship Issues Which *Love Work* Has Helped Solve

- **Addictions/Codependency:** My partner is more interested in porn/ internet games/ alcohol/ partying/

sports/ cars/ hunting/ other friends/ family, etc. than me. I don't know how to get my partner back.

- **Anxiety:** I'm always walking on egg shells around my partner. We've lost that loving feeling and don't know how to get it back.

- **Boundary Issues:** My partner smothers me, I need space. I'm attracted to someone other than my partner.

- **Communication:** We argue constantly over everything. I don't understand my partner. My partner doesn't understand me.

- **Trust:** My partner doesn't trust me no matter what I do or say. My partner had an affair, lied, or abandoned me. Now I can't forgive or trust them.

- **Emotional suppression:** My partner blows up at me for no reason. I try hard not to get angry and to be nice, then I blow up and wreck it all again.

- **Family Dynamics:** My partner spoils/ is too hard on the kids. I get stuck with all the chores.

- **Indecision:** We're on-again, off-again. We can't stabilize our relationship.

- **Resentment:** I made a mistake a long time ago. My partner will never let it go. My partner doesn't understand how much they have hurt me.

- **Unassertiveness:** My partner takes me for granted, ignores me, or talks over me. We need to make changes, but my partner is on automatic pilot.

- **Frustrations and arguments:** My partner and I argue too much about sex, money, or power.

Challenges

Some of your past experiences may make it difficult for you to learn *Love Work* skills. If so, you may find yourself needing to challenge some basic assumptions and change some old habits. Here are some of those situations:

- If you or your partner were taught to suppress or deny feelings as a child, you may not see feelings as having value, so learning to understand and respond to them may take you extra time and effort.

- If you or your partner have been traumatized by a parent or others acting out violent emotions when you were a child, you may fear dealing with feelings. So, learning these skills will take courage and possibly support from a trained counselor.

- If you or your partner habitually uses alcohol or other substances to numb emotions, your substance abuse will hamper your progress in dealing with feelings until you get your addiction under control.

- If you are keeping secrets from your partner, while pretending to be true and honest, *Love Work* is likely to make you feel increasingly uncomfortable until you deal with those secrets. (But take heart! *Love Work* also will give you skills to deal with the emotional fallout from revealing those secrets, should you choose to take that risk.)

Personal Growth

Assuming you became a couple because you love each other, you probably would like to meet each other's emotional needs. *Love Work* will give you the skills to get back on track when things happen that stress your relationship. While this approach may seem simple, it is also a powerful emotional tool. It can revitalize your relationship. At the same time, you are also likely to come face to face with sides of yourself and your partner that may make you uncomfortable. Learning to love your partner as they are, rather than as you had imagined them to be—and *vice versa*—will take personal growth and adjustment on both of your parts. However, your relationship will become vastly more interesting and enjoyable as a result.

A Broader View

The skills involved in building strong personal relationships can serve you well in a broader context as well. Many who have developed *Love Work* skills have found them useful in dealing with other family members, friends, and a variety of work relationships. The skills can be helpful in any situation in which cooperation rather that competition improves success, up to and including police work and politics.

If You Need More Than Self-Help

My intention is to give you understanding of how relationships work and to help you develop more effective relationship skills on your own. However, you learned many relationship habits and expectations very early in life and many of those operate below the level of consciousness and are difficult to change. It may take someone outside of your relationship to help you see the patterns of which you are part clearly enough for you to change them. If this approach appeals to you, but you have difficulty putting it into practice, it may be helpful for you to spend some time in counseling with a therapist specializing in relationships. You and your therapist can also use this book as an aid to your therapy.

Because it is easy to skim over a book but miss important details, focus questions are included at the end of each chapter to help you notice information you may have missed. It is a good idea to read over the questions first, before you read the chapter, so you will be looking for the answers as you go. Then review by going over the questions again after you have done the reading There are also additional helpful resources that you can read listed at the end of this book.

. This book is also a work book. It is meant to be written in, dog eared, highlighted, and generally abused. An extra page is added at the end of each chapter on which you can write comments, inspirations, and revelations as they occur to you. In this way, you can co-create your own personal copy. As you look over your comments after finishing the book, you will see how you have grown and developed. Your comments can help you get back on track years from now if you need reminders about using the relationship skills you are developing.

Focus Questions for Chapter 1

1) What 4 skill sets do you need in order to maintain a comfortable long-term relationship with your partner?

2) To master *Love Work* skills, what must you do besides read the book?

3) What are 5 expectations the *Love Work* approach assumes you would like to have for your relationship?

Notes to Myself

What Love Work Offers

Notes tp Myself

Notes to Myself

12

Chapter 2
How Relationships Work...Or Don't

Why should American Romance become American Tragedy? It doesn't have to be this way. In our culture, romantic relationships are often portrayed as being largely out of our control. The drama goes something like this: People magically fall in love. It feels it is "meant to be." They believe their love will last forever. Then unanticipated things happen that challenge that love. Couples grow apart. They can't get along. They fight, get bored, or depressed. Their spouse turns into what they hated about their parents. They get the "seven-year itch." Other people seem more exciting. The "D" word gets mentioned. Things frequently go downhill from there with trauma for all involved. Still, hope springs eternal that somewhere along the way, each wandering soul will eventually fall in love with the "right person" and make it stick. If and when this actually happens seems largely a matter of fortune.

It is true that divorce rates in the United States are high. Somewhere between thirty and fifty percent of marriages founder, and many that survive struggle along unhappily. However, some couples somehow manage to go through life mostly enjoying each other, with minimal drama and loss. They just seem to get along. How do they manage this satisfying long-term relationship that seems to elude so many?

The life of a relationship isn't really as unpredictable as it seems. Couples that understand how relationships work and have developed skills to manage them are much more likely to be among those who go through life with less pain and lots more pleasure. This chapter explains how relationships work and why they often go sour. Later chapters offer skills to get relationships back on track and keep them there.

Since people feel terrible when their intimate relationships are in trouble, the following story about getting out of Hell will illustrate good and bad relationships, and also shows an effective strategy for getting broken relationships back on track. Versions of this ancient story appear in different cultures and religions throughout the world. Everybody likes a good story!

Old Jake dies, and Saint Peter takes him around to see Heaven and Hell so that Jake can decide where he wants to spend all eternity. First, Saint Peter opens the door to Hell. Jake sees a great banquet table filled with every good and delicious food. Hungry, miserable people are sitting across from each other at the table. They can see the food. They can smell the food. But they don't have elbows. So even though they can touch the food, they cannot eat. Satisfying their craving is forever just beyond their reach.

Then Saint Peter takes Jake up to Heaven and they look in on that gathering. It's the same setup. There's a banquet table spread with great food. These people don't have elbows either, but they are all fat and happy and having a wonderful time. What's the difference? The people in heaven, of course, are feeding each other! Their conversation sounds like this:

"Here, try some of Aunt Sadie's special casserole."

"Thanks! That is great! Let me give you some too."

How Relationships Work… Or Don't

These folks in Heaven have managed to create helpful relationships with others, while those in Hell are struggling on forever alone, their relationships broken or nonexistent.

So, how do people get from the "Hell" of bad relationships to the "Heaven" of good ones? For a minute, let's return with Jake and Saint Peter back down to Hell again to view an unexpected transformation. Saint Peter points out this guy, Slim, who has been starving for all eternity. After an eternity of trying to feed himself with no elbows and never succeeding, Slim comes to the miserable realization that he is starving, and that he will always starve as long as he continues trying to feed himself. Somehow, Slim manages to put his agony on hold long enough to say to himself, "I can't feed myself, but I guess I could feed that woman across the table from me. So why not help her out a little? At least someone would feel better." He gets up his nerve, breaks with tradition, takes a spoonful of Aunt Lucille's favorite cherry pie, and gives a bite to Sally, who is sitting across the table.

Sally, who has been starving for all eternity as well, finds this quite a shock. But because she is starving, Sally eats rather than refuses the gift from the stranger across the table. What then? Sally might go on trying to feed only herself. However, now that she has become aware of a new option, Sally tries offering a bite in return. Slim is amazed to find that he is suddenly being fed, even though he had been giving food away rather than trying to feed himself! As Slim and Sally realize that they can have their needs met by feeding each other, rather than by focusing only on their own needs, they suddenly find themselves miraculously transported to the banquet in Heaven.

What made it possible for these newfound friends to switch their perspective and enter Heaven? *They discovered their ability to contain and place their own needs on hold long enough to take care of their partner's needs.* In this effort lies the secret—and the challenge— to building enduring relationships.

Human relationships are like those around that banquet table. We may try to fill the hunger of our desires with food, riches, entertainment, addictions, or other distractions, but we need the care and connection we receive from other people to fill our loneliness. Likewise, the greatest gift each of us has to bring to the table is the care and attention we can give by filling another's loneliness. We call this gift *Love.* However, there is a cost. This is the *Work* part of the *Love Work* equation. In order to reach out and fill our partners' needs, we must work to keep our own emotional hunger on hold. Fortunately, we can build our strength to do this work through practice.

How Attachment, Brain Function, and Communication Work Together in Maintaining Relationships

We begin dealing with emotions and our relationships soon after we are born. Before being born, we are used to a nice warm cozy place where our every need is met… Then unexpected things start happening! We find ourselves pushed and squeezed horribly out of shape! Then we emerge into the cold light of day and find ourselves in the rubber gloved hands of a strange being in a green suit! How do we feel? If we, as babies, had words to describe it, they would include scared, separated, out-of-control, and helpless. We don't remember this trauma because much of our infant brain is undeveloped at birth. However, the lower parts of our brain involving our amygdala and brain stem, often called our "lizard brain," which are in charge of keeping us alive, are already fully operational. These parts of our brain aren't complex or thoughtful, but they *are* fast! Triggered, they send a burst of emergency activation chemicals: noradrenaline, adrenaline and cortisol, to our brain and muscles. What do we do? We use those muscles to take a deep breath and give a helpless wail. It works! Blood circulation begins carrying oxygen from our lungs to the rest of our body. That first breath saves our life. How do we feel now? Happy and content? Nope! We are still a wreck. These parts of our brain are concerned only with our survival, not about making us feel good.

Then something else miraculous happens. A comforting voice we don't understand says, "Poor little Sweetie, you're all upset. Come to Mama." Loving arms surround us. We are held close, warmed, and fed. We reach out from that helpless panic towards this safe, loving, seemingly all-powerful being who thinks we are the cutest, most lovable thing she has ever seen or held. Our limbic system, nerves in the middle part of our brain, begin to connect and develop, patterned on the love that we are being given. Feel good chemicals oxytocin, serotonin, and dopamine are released in our brain. We start learning to regulate our emotions and feel safe, secure, and connected. Our neocortex, the top and front part of our brain involved with reason, organization, and relationships, begins making connections too. We begin to become aware that there are others in the world who can meet our needs.

These three very different brain functions, with their associated bio-chemicals and feelings, affect our relationships for the rest of our lives. We feel frightened and alone when our lizard brain is triggered. We feel calm, secure, and connected when our limbic system gives us the feeling that all is well. Our neocortex helps us build understanding of what is happening around us that is contributing to those different feelings.

These brain systems operate very differently. Our brain stem and amygdala are quick and simple. They create our fight/flight/freeze emergency reactions. When this "lizard brain" part of our brain is triggered, we tend to see things in terms of black or white, win or lose. We have to win because winning means survival. We don't worry about whether our partner loses in the process.

Our limbic brain and neocortex, on the other hand, are more complex parts of our brain that develop through our interactions with others. Our limbic brain gives us our sense of how we feel and serves as an intermediary between our lizard brain and our neocortex. Our neocortex gives us perspective, understanding, and ability to think and plan. Together, they can calm the alarms of our lizard brain and help us create solutions in which everyone involved can win. When we are functioning at these higher levels, we feel connected with others. We can imagine how others feel and think, create plans together, and work in harmony. Our lizard brain and higher brain functions are there to take care of us. However, when they are in conflict, they can make our relationships seem confusing and out of control. This is because the rules change depending on which mode of brain operation we are using.

Because our lizard brain reacts more quickly, it can flood our neocortex with noradrenalin and cortisol. These are emergency chemicals which prepare us for action but inhibit neocortical functioning. We can't act and think well at the same time. For example, when people find themselves in conflict they often, in the heat of the moment, fire off angry retorts with great power and certainty. Later, they regret what they've said, realizing too late that there were far more productive options available.

Why do people often react impulsively rather than acting thoughtfully, since poorly thought-out reactions often are counterproductive? The reason is that the parts of their brains that could have thought through to better approaches weren't engaged. In the heat of confrontation, people tend to operate in quick-draw lizard brain mode. Neocortical responses occur more slowly and operate best in a calm, nonthreatening environment. Hence, people create more effective solutions after they take time for quiet thought. This book will help you learn to use your neocortex to develop greater control over your lizard brain reactions. This skill is important for stable relationships because one partner's amygdala-driven efforts at self-protection are likely to make the other partner feel abandoned, provoking their amygdala reaction in return.

These different brain functions are related to a wide variety of different biochemical, behavioral, and psychological responses that affect our relationships. So, rather than using medical brain terms like amygdala and neocortex, I find it more useful to call our reactions related to brain stem and amygdala brain function **"Protect Mode,"** and to call our reactions related to limbic and neocortical brain function **"Connect Mode."** Differences between Protect Mode and Connect Mode are summarized in Table 1, page 28. I will use these terms rather than medical brain terms throughout this book.

Emotional Attachment: Understanding Why Relationships Are So Important

Human beings need loving social interaction and connection for the limbic system and neocortex parts of their brains to develop properly. We actively seek those connections throughout our childhood. As adults, we are drawn to the bright shining faces of the children who desire a connection with us. The love and attention we initially receive from our parents is supplemented with that which we can get from grandparents, teachers, family friends, relatives, and others who care about us as we grow up. Our brains bloom and grow as we absorb all the love we can find throughout our childhood. Through this process, our brains develop patterns of emotional regulation and expectation for our relationships that we build on throughout our lives.

When we reach adulthood, most of us begin to feel the need for a relationship with a partner through whom we can express and pass along the love that we've received. When we find that person, we make a special deal, and this deal is important! Our deal is this:

"I take care of you.
You take care of me.
We take care of each other!"

In some way, this new relationship reminds us of that deep connection we made long ago with the people who first showed us love. As in that early attachment, each of us who enters such a relationship must entrust our new partner with the tender part of ourselves that needs to be nurtured for us to feel safe and secure.

Love Lost! Why Protect Mode Takes Over

Since, at the level of our basic need for security, each of us is forever young, a new love relationship is like two children sitting as close together as they can get on an old-fashioned plank see-saw. The balance point separates their positions and their points of view. Yet they are so close that they can hold hands and share thoughts and feelings effortlessly across the gap. Communication is a cool clear stream of understanding flowing easily between them.

Sadly, because the world is an imperfect place, life intrudes in ways that threatens this easy communication. One person works nights while the other has a day shift, so they don't see each other enough. The baby is colicky and neither partner is getting enough sleep. Grim realization sets in that their partner isn't the perfection they'd expected. The partners' different approaches for dealing with problems, which may have worked well in their families growing up, cause friction in their present relationship. They find they have some conflicting values. Trust gets violated and feelings get hurt. The possibilities are endless, but what all these issues have in common is that they lack easy solutions and cause the couple to get frustrated and upset. As a result, the couple find themselves "walking on egg shells" for fear that some uncomfortable issue will rear its ugly head and stress their relationship further. It seems less threatening to put energy into avoiding these painful topics than to struggle to solve seemingly unsolvable problems.

The issues that the couple try to avoid accumulate over time. They are like rocks damming that cool clear stream of communication. Gradually they cause the easy flow of communication to slow and stop. Like water behind a dam, pressure starts to build. As the pressure grows, the couple has to put more and more energy into holding back difficult feelings. As a result, they have less and less energy available for enjoying life and having fun with each other. One might imagine this growing pressure as being an emotional balloon full of stress growing between the young couple on that see-saw, forcing them further and further apart. As their separation increases, they can no longer talk as they could in the past. The feelings of warmth and connectedness that the couple initially enjoyed are replaced by feelings of anxiety, distance, disconnection, and abandonment. They aren't holding hands across the gap between them anymore.

As the stress between them increases, the partners each descend deeper into Protect Mode and leave objective, caring Connect Mode reality further behind as well. This can begin an avalanche of changes in the couple's relationship that increases emotional pressure still more and pushes them ever deeper into Protect Mode. When couples lack the skills to shift back into Connect Mode, the accumulating emotional pain that results can leave the couple feeling lost and uncertain whether they ever really knew each other. Lovers can become strangers.

Here are some of the changes that frequently lead to this catastrophe:

A destructive new feeling appears: Anger! A partner might think, "What happened to our deal? You were going to take care of me and you're not!" Feelings like these blow up the emotional balloon still further.

Questions stop working. When partners are in Connect Mode, it is easy for them to find out what is going on with each other. They just ask, "What's wrong?" However, when one partner is in Protect Mode, questions from the other partner feel like a set up for attack from the prosecuting attorney. Then the defensive partner is likely to respond with an evasive, "Nothing is wrong, just leave me alone." This triggers Protect Mode in the other partner, as well, who thinks, "I know something is wrong and he won't tell me. Something big must be wrong!" As one partner continues to pursue with more questions, while their partner continues to evade, emotional pressure continues to build.

Perceptions get distorted. Partners are rarely aware that this is happening, but Protect Mode distorts their perceptions of each other. Since pressure increases the emotional distance between them, they see each other less clearly. Defensive communication limits their ability to get feedback that would correct their perceptions of each other. With limited information, their imaginations can run wild. Distortions can feed on past trauma they experienced growing up, memories of past relationship problems, misinformation that they have read or gleaned from the media, gossip they have heard from "friends," or any other sources, no matter how unreliable. So how does the other partner feel when one partner reacts according to these false impressions? Hurt, misjudged, and demeaned! This increases emotional pressure still more, pushing them even further apart.

Personality differences also play a role in increasing emotional pressure. Partners aren't attracted to each other simply by chance. There are likely to be many things they share in common. Perhaps they have similar values, interests, social circles, economic status, levels of intelligence and so on. However, while these are important to a smoothly running relationship, the couple is likely to take these things for granted because there are no differences that stand out. If these similar aspects of their personalities were all they shared, they would quickly grow bored with each other.

Paradoxically, an important part of the glue that holds the couple together in mutual attraction and long-term interest are the aspects of their personalities that are different but complement each other. Jess admires traits that Brian has abundantly, which Jess feels she lacks. Brian sees in Jess wonderful traits in areas where Brian feels a lack. For example, perhaps Jess is creative but disorganized, while Brian's forte is organization. Jess makes Brian's life interesting; Brian keeps Jess's life from being chaotic. Thus, because of these complementary areas, they are stronger together than either would be alone. Unfortunately, when emotional pressure builds, and the couple begins to feel separated, these same differences become liabilities. They grow into irritants that push the couple still further apart, weakening their connection. The talk between complementary personalities can degenerate into an oppositional dialogue:

"Why don't you clean up?"

"Why do you have to act like we live in a museum?"

The result of these personality conflicts is that Jess and Brian move more deeply into Protect Mode and forget the positive aspects of their differences. Soon they begin asking themselves "Why did I ever think we had anything in common?"

The rules for managing behavior turn upside down when partners enter Protect Mode. When partners are in Connect Mode, cooperation gives both partners pleasure. However, once they enter Protect Mode, cooperation feels like capitulation. Neither wants to allow their partner to win because they believe it means they themselves must lose.

In the following example, it is easy to see this how this change works in the difference between little Johnny's Connect Mode reaction to "Sweet Grandma" versus his Protect Mode reaction with "Wicked Stepmother." We adults frequently react much the same way in our intimate relationships, since at an emotional level we are all young and easily hurt.

Sweet Grandma says, "Johnny, as soon as you finish your spinach, we can have dessert!" Johnny is not fond of spinach, but, in Connect Mode, he cooperates and chokes some down to please Grandma… and to get a piece of her famous fresh strawberry cheese cake.

On the other hand, Wicked Stepmother snarls, "Johnny, if you don't eat that spinach, you're not getting any dessert!" While the behavior desired and the reward is the same, in this case, the spinach isn't likely go anywhere without a struggle. In Protect Mode, Johnny may prefer to starve rather than give his stepmother the satisfaction of seeing him cave in to her demands. Most people react similarly in their willingness to cooperate when their partners begin to feel like adversaries.

Winning at one's partner's expense becomes motivating when increasing emotional pressure causes us to move into Protect Mode. Mutually destructive behavioral cycles are likely to result. If Nick works toward winning at Ashley's expense, then Ashley, not enjoying being the loser, will also move into Protect Mode and struggle to win at Nick's expense in return. As this cycle continues, most of their energy is spent in struggle with each other rather than in enjoying progress through life together. Couples caught in these Protect Mode reaction cycles spend a great deal of time feeling exhausted, helpless, frustrated, angry, abandoned, and out of control.

Protect Mode vs Connect Mode: A Comparison

Even though couples are much happier and more effective when they operate in Connect Mode, once they fall into Protect Mode reaction patterns, it can be difficult for them to find their way back out of ingrained reactive habits. This leads to our high divorce rate and a lot of wasted time and energy.

Satisfying relationships operate mostly in Connect Mode, with each member of the couple finding pleasure in taking care of their partner. So how do couples make the switch back to Connect Mode once emotional pressure has gotten too high and they get stuck in Protect Mode?

Here are two conversations. Each starts with the same Protect Mode question. One escalates into ever-increasing emotional pressure. The other winds down to calm and reconnection. Can you tell what makes the difference?

A Protect Mode reaction cycle between partners might go something like this:

"Why do you have to argue with everything I say?"

"Why do you have to be so opinionated about every little thing?"

"There you go again!"

"What are you talking about? You started it!"

"I did not start it! I'm just trying to get you to shut up and give me some peace."

"If you want peace so badly, why do you always have to have the last word?"

...etc., ad infinitum...

It is exhausting just to write this example down. It is even harder to live it.

In contrast, let's look at a Connect Mode conversation. Here, one of the partners is having a bad day and attacks with the same angry initial question that began the Protect Mode argument in the last paragraph. However, in this case, the other partner, rather than reacting in Protect Mode, manages to stay calm and "reaches across the table to feed his partner" by seeking to understand his angry partner's point of view. In the process he lowers the emotional pressure his partner carries, so that she can feel calm and safe, and begin to reconnect:

"Why do you have to argue with everything I say?"

"Hmm... Sounds like I really irritated you when I disagreed that Global Warming is a hoax.

"Well, you know it might be. Weather changes all the time."

"It is really important to you that I at least hear you out even if I don't agree."

"Yes, I really appreciate it when you let me share my thoughts.

"I can tell it makes you feel better when I'm listening.

"Yes... It makes me feel warm and safe... Thanks for being there for me."

Table 1
Protect Mode _vs_ Connect Mode Functioning

Function	Protect Mode	Connect Mode
Brain	Brain Stem, Amygdala	Limbic System, Neocortex
Response	Fight, flight, freeze	Connect, cooperate
Feeling	Anxious, angry, alone, defensive	Secure, happy, capable
Attachment	Lost, abandoned	Found, loved
Perception	Distorted, subjective	Clear, objective
Identity	"Me" focus	"We" focus
Communication	Push own agenda, distrust other's input, questions seen as attacks, discount other points of view	Work with partner's point of view, respond openly to questions, build mutual understanding
Problem Solving	Simple all-or-nothing solutions. "I have to win, your loss is OK. My needs are most important."	Complex win/ win solutions are most important. All participants' needs are important.
Relationship	Power-oriented	Connection-oriented
Personality	Differences are irritating. "Why can't you be like me?"	Differences are welcome. "How can we use them to build new ideas?"
Behavior	Oppositional, punishment oriented: "Wicked Stepmother's Rule"	Cooperative, reward oriented: "Grandma's Rule"
Focus	Rigid	Flexible
Biochemical	Cortisol, Adrenalin, Noradrenalin	Oxytocin, Serotonin, Dopamine
Physiological	Tensed, stressed	Relaxed, comfortable
Reaction	Impulsive, reactive	Thoughtful, deliberate
Energy	Deficit	Surplus

Focus Questions for Chapter 2

1) What basic ability do people need to develop to be able to maintain enduring personal relationships?

2) How can we tell when we are operating in Protect Mode?
How can we tell when we are operating in Connect Mode?

3) What changes often occur when we are in Protect Mode that can cause relationships under stress to avalanche towards collapse?

4) What is the Basic Deal we must negotiate with our partner in order to enter a committed relationship?

What's Next

Love Work offers paths out of the Protect Mode maze. In Chapter 3, you will learn skills to:
1) lower the emotional pressure you carry in your relationship,
2) build mutual understanding between you and your partner, and
3) reconnect with your partner at a deeper emotional level.

Notes to Myself

32

Notes to Myself

33

Dealing With Emotional Pressure
Low Pressure
The Deal
I take Care of You! You Take Care of Me!
We take Care of Each Other!

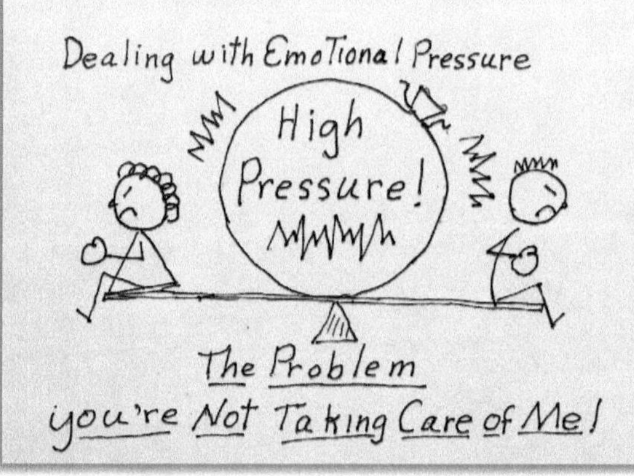

Dealing with Emotional Pressure
High Pressure!
The Problem
you're Not Taking Care of Me!

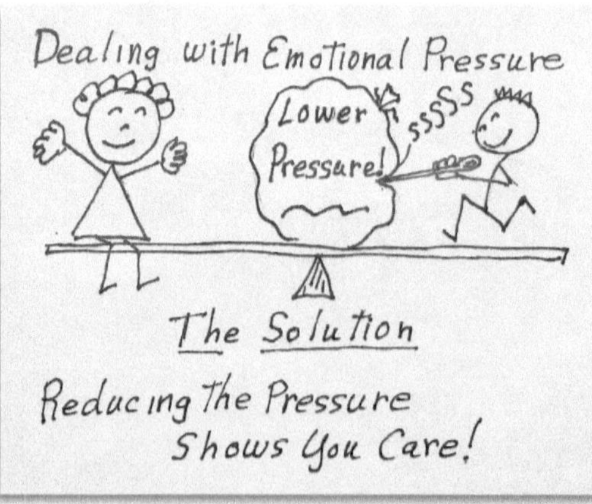

Dealing with Emotional Pressure
Lower Pressure!
The Solution
Reducing The Pressure
Shows You Care!

Chapter 3
Introducing Your Search Path:
Break Hurtful Patterns and Reconnect

Since Protect Mode interactions often avalanche into relationship disasters, couples feel safer and more in control if they have tools available to get out of Protect Mode and back into Connect Mode. Then they can resume the happy, productive life together that they desire.

Couples in distress often resort to a variety of futile strategies to recapture their lost connection. While these approaches may work when couples are in Connect Mode, they often cause problems to continue once the couple enters Protect Mode. Among many others, these strategies include: attempts at problem solving, analyzing personality weaknesses, rehashing a litany of offenses, defending themselves, apologizing, bringing up childhood trauma, deciding who was right or wrong, and asking questions about the problem. In spite of these efforts, couples continue feeling upset, alone, and caught in Protect Mode interactions. They are discouraged. They have tried everything, and nothing works!

Surprisingly, these same couples will discover they can reconnect when they learn to focus instead on reducing the emotional pressure that is holding them apart and isolated, rather than trying to solve problems that have no resolution. Couples can reduce this pressure by persevering with a single task: *Guess your partner's feelings and your partner's reasons for those feelings. Then listen!* Continue to do this for each other until each partner feels heard and understood.

Why does this work? When we were very young, our parents used a series of trial-and-error guesses to figure out how we were feeling and why we might be feeling that way so that they could take care of our needs. Since we could not yet talk, our parents had to use the following thought process to discover what our problem was: "My baby is crying. I guess he must be unhappy. Why might that be? Maybe he is hungry… No, he won't eat. Maybe he's bored… No, entertainment doesn't help. Maybe he's sleepy… No, He won't go to sleep. Maybe his diaper needs changing… Whoops! There's the problem. I can take care of that."

Our parents used this process because they cared enough about us to try to determine what was wrong and how to meet our needs. As a result, we have learned to react with a sense of security and calm when we recognize that someone desires to understand us and take care of us. Our brain gets a nice burst of oxytocin and it makes us feel good, so we let go of the emotional pressure we carry and relax. Since all of us went through these experiences as children, this emotional response is common to us all. So, now that we are adults, we can still offer this same concerned care to our partners to calm them down, and our partners can do the same for us. When we put our own needs and concerns on hold for a while and instead pay attention to our partners' needs and respond to them, our partners begin to feel cared for and understood. Like children who have been comforted, our partners also become more able to let go of the emotional pressure they carry and return from Protect Mode to their Connect Mode of functioning.

There is a difference, of course. As adults, we need to approach our partners more cautiously, using words at first, since we all have developed potent defenses over the years. Angry porcupines can't just settle their differences with a hug.

The Problem with Feelings

Notice, though, that this means recognizing, respecting, and standing calmly in the presence of our partner's feelings. Unfortunately, feelings can be problematic.

First, they are invisible. We know when we have them, but we can't directly experience those that someone else is holding. We can only infer what others' feelings might be, and our inferences can easily be mistaken.

Second, feelings can quickly change. An infant can be crying one moment and happy and contented a short time later. The same can be true for us. Just when we think we know what is going on with our partner, we may be frustrated to learn our partner's feelings now have changed to something different.

Third, our partner's feelings can hurt us. If our partner directs their anger towards us, we are likely to get upset as well, making things still worse.

Finally, we can deny feelings and pretend they don't exist, both in ourselves and in our partners. This last problem with feelings can be dangerous. Let's look at it more closely.

Most of us have heard as children, and have said to others in turn, statements that dismiss or harshly judge feelings, such as: "Don't be such a cry baby!" or "If you can't say something nice, don't say anything at all!" As a result, we often hide feelings we consider unacceptable and put our energy into smiling politely and doing what we think is expected of us. As we work hard to pretend certain feelings don't exist, we often fool everyone, including ourselves, and become isolated from our own feelings as well as from those that others may be carrying. Because we have no control over feelings we are unaware of, the more we deny feelings, the crazier things can get. When people try to avoid feelings altogether, emotional pressure can build high enough for emotions to explode into action with unpredictable results.

For example, here is a tale which may have some basis in fact, that I heard as a child in which feelings were not dealt with at all. Depression-era Covesville, Virginia, was a small place without much going on, so truth was rarely allowed to stand in the way of a good story. Names have been changed to protect the guilty:

Curtis and Ruby had been married for a while and they weren't getting along too well. In those days of crank telephones and party lines, word gets around, and Curtis had heard rumor that Ruby had got herself a boyfriend on the side. Curtis decided to find out for sure. Saturday morning, he told Ruby he was going out squirrel hunting and would be back by dark. He headed out the door with a .22 rifle and a flask in his pocket. But instead of heading up the mountain, Curtis circled around, settled back in the bushes near the house, and waited. He hadn't drunk more than half the flask when a fancy Model A Ford rolled up and a fella he didn't know climbed out. Ruby met the fella on the porch with a warm embrace. Curtis took careful aim and pulled the trigger. However, Curtis missed the fella and hit Ruby by mistake. The fella took off in a hurry. Fortunately, Curtis missed anything vital. So, Ruby put a Band-Aid on her front where the bullet went in, and another on her back where the bullet came out. In a few weeks she got all right and Curtis and Ruby never had any more trouble.

Notice there are no feelings offered in this story. It is all about action. That doesn't mean feelings didn't exist. Emotional pressure must have gotten pretty high for Ruby to turn to another man, and for Curtis to settle the problem with a squirrel rifle. The story ends with assurances of no more trouble. It doesn't say anyone was feeling relaxed or happy. Curtis probably continued to feel jealous and insecure. Ruby probably continued to feel lonely and afraid of her husband.

So, while we often treat feelings as an awkward inconvenience, an immature remnant of ourselves which we hope will go away, feelings do not vanish on command. When they are ignored, emotional pressure continues to build with all the Protect Mode problems previously described increasing as well.

Negative feelings might be described as a canary in the coal mine, warning of impending danger. Rather than trying to hide or change feelings in ourselves or others, we do better when we focus on calmly guessing what they are and why they might be occurring, just as our parents did for us when we were infants long ago. Then feelings calm and become positive forces for connection and safety in our lives.

For many of us, as for Curtis and Ruby, awareness of feelings has not been much a part of our adult lives. Because of this, we may have a very narrow feeling vocabulary that we recognize as applying to ourselves or our partners. Some people admit few feelings because their social environment encourages action rather than feelings. *Angry, excited, relaxed,* and *tired* may represent the entire feeling repertoire for some. However, when the few feelings that that they do admit are heard and respected, people begin to let their guards down and discover more vulnerable feelings that they may be willing to share.

The feelings we accept are the ones we have control over. The ones we deny tend to grow, increasing emotional pressure until we have to release them somehow, perhaps by acting them out through a fight, going on a binge, or having an affair. Other unfortunate results of repressed feelings include getting depressed, getting divorced, having a heart attack, or even killing someone. *Love Work* skills can ease emotional pressure, allowing us to recognize and accept the feelings we and our partners carry and gain some control over them.

There are a multitude of emotions that couples can try on for size. Any choice will do as long as we attach a reason for the feeling that makes sense to us and our partner:

Here are some negative feelings we might be carrying when emotional pressure is high: sad… stressed out… anxious… scared… terrified… horrified … shy… bewildered… cautious… hurt… disparaged… lonely… disrespected… out of control… suspicious… jealous… depressed… longing… repulsed… pissed off… discontent… agitated… dependent… enraged… outraged… hateful… hesitant… harried… rushed… overwhelmed… insecure… unappreciated… blamed… covetous… hostile… stingy… ashamed… lustful… taken for granted… angry… entitled… hopeless… bored… disconnected… tired… vengeful… confused… embarrassed… furious… drained.

Here are some positive feelings we may experience once emotional pressure has been lowered: happy… glad… content… joyful… confident… calm… serene… full of anticipation… hopeful… loving… generous… alive… energized… thankful… peaceful… fulfilled… respected… honored… glad… generous… connected… silly… relaxed… independent… excited… stimulated… thoughtful… surprised… grateful… playful.

We might look at positive feelings as similar to oil in the works of an antique clock. The oil isn't actually part of the clock, but it is essential for its many gears to move smoothly with each other. When feelings are respected and honored as important parts of our relationship, they become positive forces that help us work smoothly together as well. When feelings are denied and neglected, pressure builds, friction develops, and the gears of our relationships begin to seize up and break down.

So, managing feelings is essential to maintaining relaxed, comfortable long-term relationships. But given that feelings, like oil, are slippery things that are hard to grasp, how can we actually achieve this with people we care about and with whom we are living in close contact?

The Problem with Questions

One obvious strategy that people use to open the topic of feelings is simply to ask a question: "Is something wrong?" or "What's bothering you?" This approach works fine when emotional pressure is low and both partners are operating in Connect Mode. However, when emotional pressure has built up and partners have moved into Protect Mode, paradoxically, the reverse of what we intend can easily happen.

When a person who feels vulnerable hears such questions from the person they see as involved in their discomfort, their anxiety is likely to increase. If Jill asks such a question, Sam may worry that Jill will judge him negatively for having negative feelings about her. He may worry that he will hurt Jill's feelings and damage their relationship still further. As a result, Sam is likely to react to a question in Protect Mode, by denying that anything is wrong, or by asking to be left alone. These flight responses tend to leave the partner who asked the question feeling put off and alone in return. So, Jill's Protect Mode reaction gets triggered too.

The other frequent reaction to questions from a person in Protect Mode is a fight response. In a blast of pressure release, Sam may lash out with an attack such as, "You are the problem!" This is likely to trigger Jill's Protect Mode as well, either starting a fight or sending Jill into full retreat. In either case, the problem remains. So, while we may be asking our partner questions out of genuine concern, using questions as a method of dealing with relationship problems often works against us, raising the pressure and widening rather than closing the emotional gap we have been experiencing. This shuts down communication still further.

Rebuilding Emotional Connections: The Search Path

A very specific sequence of guesses works much better for repairing relationships than posing questions does. Why is this? When Jill, who is feeling OK, asks questions of her emotionally upset partner, Sam, she is asking Sam to take the risk that Jill may reject what he tells her. This would make Sam feel still worse. On the other hand, when Jill makes a guess about Sam's feelings, she, rather than Sam, is taking the risk. Since Jill feels OK to start with, she has less to lose. Doing this can be trickier than it sounds. There is potential for both partners to wind up feeling badly, with no emotional gain for anyone.

But, you can learn to use guesses safely and productively. In *Love Work* we call this process our **Search Path**. Here, we use a series of guesses to calm and gain a deeper understanding of our partner. People in any sort of mutual relationship can use Search Path skills to create an effective dialogue for calming and clarifying emotional issues between them.

Following one's Search Path may seem obvious and easy to do, but it takes practice. It requires us to base our understanding on the information our partner gives us in the present moment, rather than responding to our preconceived ideas about our partner. It takes self-discipline to attend our partner's feelings and seek to gain deeper understanding of them, no matter where they go, rather than trying to control or change their feelings. It means operating on the assumption that our partner has good reasons for their feelings and their behavior, even if we do not yet understand them. It means steadily attending our partner's point of view rather than switching back to our own.

As we try to accommodate the new information that our partner gives us in our follow-up guesses, we convince our partner that we really are interested in their point of view and that we really do care about them. If our partner's feelings veer off onto another topic, our job is to follow along with our guesses. If our partner's feelings go in uncomfortable directions for us, we need to take a deep breath, relax, and continue to follow along despite our discomfort. Our chance to relieve our own discomfort will come later, after we have finished our job of calming and caring for our partner.

Let's look at how to actually use your Search Path.

The Steps to Your Search Path:

1) Stop, take a deep breath, and relax… Notice where in your body you are feeling tense and relax that, too. Doing this activates your limbic brain system. Give yourself a moment to think about what is going on with your partner. This involves using your neocortex. Doing these two things helps you move out of your own Protect Mode and gives you some time to allow your Connect Mode to function.

2) A) Guess to yourself a word or short phrase that describes how your partner might be feeling. Again, this connects you to the limbic system of your brain.
    B) Guess to yourself a reasonable explanation why your partner might be feeling that way. Again, this requires you to connect with your neocortex.

3) State your guess to your partner in a calm voice. Maintain eye contact. Be sure to include *both* a Name for the feeling *and* the Reason for that feeling. Keep it short. Doing this encourages your partner to connect to their limbic system and neocortex as well.

4) Stop talking, wait, and listen to your partner's feedback. Be sure to notice corrections or reactions that your partner makes to either part of your guess. As you show yourself willing to be open to your partner's input, your partner will get a nice dose of oxytocin and begin to relax.

5) Go back to Step 1 and repeat the process based on the new information your partner has given you. Continue this process until your partner feels relaxed, heard, and understood. The nice thing about the feel-good chemical, oxcytocin, is that it is a shared brain chemical. As your partner begins feeling better, your own body responds by giving you an oxytocin burst, too.

The Benefits of The Search Path

- You gain a better understanding of your partner's emotional world and viewpoint.

- Your partner trusts you more because you have invested time and attention in the relationship, giving evidence that you care.

- As your partner feels heard and understood, they begin to join you in calm Connect Mode.

- As your partner relaxes, they become more receptive to your point of view as well.

- You increase in emotional maturity as you practice and develop the skill of putting your own needs on hold while seeking to understand your partner.

- Your relationship becomes less volatile and reactive and grows more calm, reflective, and enjoyable.

- You both increase in confidence that your relationship is more important than your differences.

Practice *Love Work* Skills
To Make Them Yours

Simply understanding these strategies may help some, but this is probably not the way you usually communicate. It will be important for you to build new brain circuits by practicing skill building exercises until you can use these skills without having to think about how to do them. Even though you may find them somewhat awkward at first, take time to play the *Love Work* games offered. Then you will be able to use the skills easily in real situations that affect your relationship.

You will find your first skill development game after the focus questions at the end of Chapter 3.

Focus Questions for Chapter 3

1) Name some common problem-solving approaches that stop working when couples move into Protect Mode.

2) What is an approach couples can use to get out of Protect Mode so that usual problem-solving skills will begin working again?

3) Why does asking questions about feelings often stop working when one's partner is in Protect Mode?

4) What is the Search Path process? What are its benefits?

Love Work Game for Chapter 3:

Here is a situation with which you can try out Search Path skills with your partner or an interested friend. Make up a conversation in which you talk through the situation described using your Search Path. Next, trade places and try the conversation again, so you both get to play each role.

Keep notes on your interactions:

Your partner spends breakfast looking at Facebook on their smart phone. They get irritated when you say you would like breakfast to be a time for conversation and connection.

1. For this situation, make your first Search Path guess to begin calming your partner.

A (feeling)_______________________________________

B (reason)_______________________________________

What is your partner's response to your Search Path statement?

____

____

Based on that response, what is your follow up Search Path statement?

A (feeling)_______________________________________

B (reason)_________________________________

What did you learn from your partner that you
weren't aware of before?

____

____

How will that affect your next Search Path
statement?

____

____

How did this exchange affect your partner's feelings
concerning the original problem?

____

____

2. Write down your partner's first *Search Path* guess
when it is their turn to try calming you.
A (feeling) _________________________________
B (reason) _________________________________
How do you respond? _________________________________

____

____

3. What is your partner's follow up Search Path
statement based on your response?
A (feeling) _________________________________

____

B (reason) _______________________________

____

What did your partner learn from you that they weren't aware of before?

____

____

How does this affect their follow up Search Path statement?

____

____

4. How does this exchange affect your feelings concerning the original problem?

____

____

____

What's Next?

Using our Search Path seems reasonable and has lots of benefits. So why don't people use it regularly? The problem is that we need to be in our Connect Mode to use it. As soon as we hear things we don't like, we automatically flip into our own Protect Mode and forget about our Search Path. Chapter 4 will help you become more aware of your own Protect Mode reactions and how to get them under your control.

Notes to Myself

51

Notes to Myself

52

Chapter 4
Managing Your Protect Mode

We have all heard the exasperated saying, "Don't just stand there, do something!" The White Rabbit in Disney's version of *Alice in Wonderland* turns that statement on its head as he shouts: "Don't just *do* something, *stand* there!" This change fits the *Love Work* approach nicely. To use our Search Path effectively, we need to stop and think carefully *before* we act. While our Protect Mode can help save us from real threats, it can also cause real damage when it interferes with our relationships. In this chapter, we will look at quick Protect Mode reactions that we must learn to calm and hold onto in order to use our Search Path effectively.

Why Using Our Search Path
Can Be Challenging

The Search Path seems simple and has great benefits. So why don't people operate this way automatically? The approach doesn't come naturally because over the years we have all developed a variety of quick Protect Mode reactions to ward off potential attack or discomfort. Our natural, amygdala-driven desire to protect ourselves produces thoughts like, "Hey! I've got feelings too! You should be taking care of me!" Having our needs met first would be nice, but we have direct control only over our own behavior. We are not in control of our partner's actions. When our partners are in

Protect Mode, they would rather take care of themselves than cooperate to meet our needs. So, in order to have influence over our relationships, we'd best use a tool we can directly control, our own behavior, rather than trying to make our partners control theirs.

Using our Search Path sounds reasonable and it works well, but it does take some courage and self-discipline. To use it, we have to learn to calm our own Protect Mode reactions even when we are irritated or worried by our partner's behavior. Once we enter full blown Protect Mode, we forget Connect Mode, and lose interest in having any better understanding of our unpleasant partner. In that state, we think we already know all we need to know about our partner: They are a jerk!

Even when we manage to restrain our initial Protect Mode "I want you to take care of me first!" reaction, we are likely to be unaware of other Protect Mode behaviors we use that maintain our relationship difficulties. For example, we may try to escape the situation or attempt to make our partner change their behavior. Either of these defensive reactions on our part will leave our partner feeling abandoned and stuck in their Protect Mode.

Following our Search Path means we must try to guess how our partner is feeling, and we may not have a clue. Here, our own Protect Mode is likely to kick in again. If we guess wrong, we fear that our partner will get still more upset, and besides, nobody enjoys being corrected. We like to be right! We expose some of who we are to our partner when we make a guess at how our partner looks at things. The risk of being wrong or rejected increases our own sense of vulnerability to attack.

As we listen to our partner, we may find ourselves uncomfortable with the feelings our partner is describing. Our intentions may be good. We simply wish to alleviate our partner's pain. Because we love our partner, we are hurting if our partner is hurting. So, we fall into Protect Mode again and try to change our partner's feelings by inserting our own perspective. We are just trying to help. Unfortunately, when we divert our attention from our partner's feelings by interrupting with our own point of view, we often leave our partner feeling even more irritated, abandoned, and misunderstood. *Remember, our goal at this point is reconnection, rather than solving all our partner's problems.* We can manage this best by doing the hard work of standing calmly in the presence of our partner's pain, rather than trying to apply quick band-aids to make their pain go away.

To use our Search Path effectively, first we must gently calm our own Protect Mode reactions and put them on hold temporarily while we continue to track and respect our partner's feelings. We are most effective when we learn to stick to our Search Path even when we may personally disagree with what we are hearing or find it uncomfortable. As we hear our partner out, we create receptive conditions in which our partner becomes willing to listen to our perspective in return. This takes the self-discipline to endure some pain to ease our partner's pain first, before trying to meet our own needs. We cannot pay attention to our own needs and our partner's needs at the same time. *It is this effort that we put into containing our own Protect Mode reactions, while we attend our partner's thoughts and feelings, that reduces the negative emotional pressure that separates us and allows us to reconnect.*

Below are examples of Protect Mode and Connect Mode conversations showing how the different brain processes operate. Notice, as well, the different outcomes that are likely to occur. First is an example of a Protect Mode conversation. John has good intentions, and he really wants to understand why Emily is so upset. But he forgets what he has learned about Protect Mode and Connect Mode, and the conversation goes in a direction that he doesn't intend:

John: "Honey, what's wrong?" (A question sets him up for an attack.)

Emily: "Don't call me 'Honey' when you leave me a trashed kitchen!" (Emily has been having a rough day. She is in Protect Mode and lets off emotional pressure by attacking him.)

John: "Oh, sorry about that." (John moves into a Protect Mode flight response: he tries to escape by apologizing.)

Emily: "Don't sorry me! You never follow through with anything you promise." (Emily doesn't feel heard, so, still in Protect Mode, she vents emotional pressure with another attack.)

John: "Now Honey, don't get upset over a few dirty dishes." (He tries to escape by minimizing her feelings: another Protect Mode escape strategy.)

Emily: "Don't get upset! Why shouldn't I get upset? You don't care about me! You don't hear me! Then you lie and call me Honey!" (Now Emily feels not only unheard, but now John is denying her feelings as well. This increases emotional pressure still further, so she attacks still harder.)

John: "Well, you're no angel yourself! The kids are out of control, you spend your life stuck on that smartphone and do nothing but complain about me!" (Escape did not work. So, still in Protect Mode after feeling attacked and wounded three times, John moves into a fight response and tries to out-yell Emily.)

At this point John and Emily are likely to continue attacking each other, with emotional pressure pushing them deeper into a major fight. Finally, bruised and exhausted, and still caught in Protect Mode, they will probably retreat into stony silence, emotional pressure at the bursting point, both walking on eggshells, both avoiding dealing with feelings, and both fearing the next explosion.

In contrast, when at least one partner remembers to use their Search Path, a much more constructive Connect Mode conversation is likely to result. As discussed earlier, rather than asking questions, we can begin a more effective conversation by first taking a breath or two and calming ourselves, remembering that a more productive approach involves investing in our partner's feelings first. Then we guess how we think our partner might be feeling, and why our partner might be feeling that way. After we make this shot in the dark, we wait calmly for feedback from our partner. Human nature is fairly predictable. Even though our partner may not have been paying attention to their feelings at the moment, they are likely to respond to a Search Path guess by taking a look inside and deciding how they actually do feel, if only to correct our misperceptions.

Here is a successful Connect Mode conversation in which John remembers to use his Search Path:

John: "Honey, you seem really stressed out. Things must have been rough at work today…." (John begins his Search Path by guessing how he thinks Emily is feeling and why he thinks she feels that way. Then he waits patiently for feedback.)

Emily: "Well, not exactly . . . I was preoccupied thinking about how tight money is. In the process, I ran a stoplight and got a $200 ticket on top of everything else." (She corrects John's guess and emotional pressure reduces a little.)

John: "No wonder you seem stressed. You were worried about our finances, and getting a ticket made you feel even worse. Now you are angry at yourself for getting the ticket, as well as being worried." (John adjusts his guess about Emily's feelings and why she has them, based on her response. Then he waits for additional feedback.)

Emily: "I'm not really angry at myself, I'm more upset with you for quitting your job and leaving all the money problems in my lap." (She corrects John and begins to deal with issues between them.)

This is where emotional communication is likely to break down. At this point John may feel attacked and want to leave his Search Path. His impulse would be to move into his own Protect Mode and retort: "Well, you agreed that I should put time into starting my own business. You knew it would be hard for a while!" Unfortunately, this approach, while it might seem reasonable and justified, will just rebuild pressure in the emotional balloon standing between them that John has been attempting to reduce. Emily will feel abandoned because John has stopped attending her feelings in order to protect his own. So, such an approach is likely to shut down communication or start a fight. John will do better if he takes a deep breath, calms himself down and puts his own point of view on hold for a while longer, knowing that he can pick his own perspective up later, after Emily has become calm and receptive.

So, for now John relaxes back into Connect Mode and resumes his Search Path.

John: "It sounds like you are beginning to regret taking on this load. It seems more than you can handle." (John again names Emily's feelings and reasons she might be feeling that way, based on her last response.

Emily: "You are so right about that!" (Emily responds by affirming his guess.)

John: "Tell me more." (John senses the pressure between them lowering with his acceptance of Emily's negative feelings. He invites Emily to let it reduce further.)

Emily: "I'm tired, John. I don't think I can keep this up." (As pressure reduces, Emily moves beyond anger and feels safe enough to admit her exhaustion. She is beginning to reconnect.)

John: "It sounds like you've been trying really hard and are worn out. You just don't see how we can make ends meet. You wish I were still working." (John's guess reflects Emily's emotional movement beyond her upset feelings toward what she is yearning for instead.)

Notice what happens as John puts his own concerns aside for the time being and focuses on Emily's feelings and the reasons she might have them. John learns to understand her more fully. Emily feels understood and understands herself more clearly. The emotional pressure Emily carries reduces, allowing her to calm down and reconnect.

Another advantage to the Search Path is that it can help protect John from attack. As Emily begins to focus internally on her own feelings, rather than externally on John as the source of the problem, he ceases to be the target of her frustration and becomes instead a partner in the problem's solution.

At this point, because Emily feels heard and understood, she becomes receptive to John's point of view as well. This engages them in a calm state of mutual connection. We can call it "We-dom." In this state, the couple can cooperate comfortably as they develop mutually acceptable solutions for whatever issues have been stressing them out. You can tell when couples are operating at this level of connection because they refer to themselves as a team: "These are what <u>our</u> hopes are....", "Here is what <u>we</u> plan to do...," etc.

In A Nutshell

A couple's ability to communicate and cooperate decreases as emotional pressure builds, so common sense approaches to problem resolution stop working. This is because human brains operate differently in defensive Protect Mode than they do in cooperative Connect Mode. Hence our first job in communication with our partner is to reduce the emotional pressure that exists between us, so we can reconnect. Communication doesn't happen until we have a connection. An effective tool for doing this is the Search Path process: First, we calm ourselves down and try to imagine what our partner's perspective is. Then, from our calm space, we state this perspective by guessing how our partner might be feeling and why our partner might be feeling that way. Finally, we adjust and restate our guess again and again, based on the feedback we receive from our partner, until our partner feels heard and understood. As we use this process, emotional pressure reduces. Our partner calms down and becomes more receptive to our point of view as well.

Briars in Our Search Path

While using our Search Path is easy enough when we are calm and in Connect Mode, when we hear thoughts or feelings from our partner that make us uncomfortable, our own Protect Mode is likely to get triggered. Then we are likely to forget our Search Path and react in ways that hurt our efforts to calm our partner. Suddenly, we find that we have left our Search Path and gotten caught in a briar patch of old Protect Mode habits.

Here are some common briars that can block Search Path efforts:

The Searcher offers a quick apology to solve the problem: "Oh, sorry about that!" This is a quick and easy way to avoid an issue. Since an apology has been offered, there is nothing else to discuss. If their partner tries to continue to talk about the issue, they may fear they will be met with a more intense Protect Mode response such as, "Look. I apologized! What else do you want?" Hence, the subject is likely to get dropped and emotional pressure will remain. An apology may be in order at some point in the conversation, but only after feelings have been explored and pressure has been reduced.

The Searcher only gives half the message when they try to use their Search Path. Either they state how they think their partner is feeling, without giving a reason, or they focus on reasons without remembering to guess their partner's feelings. Unfortunately, half messages don't work very well. They are like receiving a bowl without soup, or soup without a bowl. A good meal requires both. Focusing only on emotions without providing a reason for those feelings may well increase rather than decrease their partner's emotional intensity.

This is likely to cause the Searcher to get anxious and give up on their Search Path attempt.

On the other hand, a partner who focuses on reasons without naming the emotions involved will appear to be caught up in their own ideas rather than focusing on the other person. This leaves their partner sensing that their feelings aren't important. As a result, emotional pressure remains high and their difficult emotions continue.

Using both halves of the Search Path message, guessing our partner's feelings *together* with the reason for their emotions, helps our partner integrate the emotional and the intellectual parts of their brain. It shows our upset partner that we really are present and willing to share their total experience. They will feel calmer and more under control when they realize that the emotions they are experiencing make sense.

For example, saying either "I think you are mad" or "I forgot our dinner date" is not likely to calm our partner and open a conversation. We will do better at rebuilding our relationship when we combine feeling with reason by guessing, "I think you are mad because I forgot our dinner date." Now a conversation about feelings rather than an argument can occur.

The Searcher gives a general response to feedback about his guess without showing he heard specific details: For instance, the Searcher might guess, "You're upset because I screwed up." Hearing this, the Responder may not feel heard, or may not believe the Searcher is invested in the conversation. The Searcher will do better by showing that he heard the details of the feedback he received in his next guess. A more detailed response might be, "It sounds like you are irritated with me because I overdrew our bank account and we're stuck with an overdraft penalty."

The Searcher reflects his partner's point of view adequately, but then adds a "but" and counters that view with his own. Since the second action negates the first, emotional pressure will remain. Here is an example: "It sounds like I hurt your feelings, but you made me mad!" The Searcher needs to hold on to their "buts" and do one thing at a time. They will have a chance to express their point of view <u>after</u> they have first taken the time to carefully hear their partner out.

The Searcher tries to change their partner's intense emotions by minimizing them. Things work better when the Searcher overstates his guess about the intensity of his partner's emotions. Then his partner can correct him towards her calmer state. If the Searcher minimizes his partner's emotions, his partner will feel she has to express her feelings even more intensely to get the idea across. For example: Alicia might ask, "What kind of father are you to forget your child's birthday?!" If Kevin gives a minimizing Search Path response, such as, "You are a little upset because I forgot Johnny's birthday," then he will invite a still more angry response because Kevin still doesn't get what a big deal it was. On the other hand, if Kevin overstates Alicia's emotions in his response, he is likely to get a calmer "It's not that bad" reaction. For example, if Kevin had responded, "You are furious with me because I forgot Johnny's birthday party," Alicia's response would likely have been a calmer, "Well Johnny was really disappointed and so was I. You really blew it!"

The Searcher tries to avoid criticism by moving to the passive mood in his response: Julia might guess, "You think mistakes were made," rather than, "You think I made mistakes." Here, Julia isn't owning her responsibility for the problem. By using the passive tense Julia is implying that circumstances or other people rather than herself may have caused the situation. As a result, Jeff, who thinks Julia caused the problem, will not feel heard and emotional tension will remain. Julia would do better by recognizing the responsibility Jeff gives her by using the "I" word in her next guess, regardless of whether she agrees or not.

A partner may attempt to deflect the anxiety they are feeling by complaining about the other partner to third parties, rather than talking directly to each other about their concerns. This can relieve personal pressure, but it does not lower the pressure within the couple. In fact, it is likely to make things worse if one partner feels excluded or ganged up on. When Jim realizes he and his partner have fallen into this pattern of triangulation, Jim can get the conversation back on track by using his Search Path and telling Rick how he thinks Rick might be feeling and why Rick might be feeling that way. Jim might say, "You sounded critical of me with the comment you made to our friends last night. Maybe you are frustrated that I have been gaining weight and haven't been exercising like I should…"

Sometimes the responding partner gives a short response that doesn't give the Searching partner enough information to modify his guess. The Searcher can use three magic words to get the conversation moving again: "Tell me more."

On the other hand, the Searcher's efforts may encourage the responding partner to let go an endless barrage of complaints and emotions. If Megan is giving too much information for Sam to keep up with, it is important for Sam to slow Megan down to manageable pieces of communication. Otherwise, Sam will wind up feeling overwhelmed and move into Protect Mode as well. Then Megan won't sense that Sam has actually been hearing her.

Sam can do this by breaking into Megan's monologue with the comment, "Let me see if I understand you so far." Sam can then proceed to describe his understanding concerning how Megan is feeling and why she might be feeling that way. Even though Sam interrupts Megan to make his guess, Megan still will feel better understood and her emotional tension reduced. Sam is not cutting Megan off. He is simply reflecting bite-sized pieces of what Megan is trying to express.

The conversation gets stuck on negative feelings. Sometimes the Searcher's efforts can lead to an endless recitation of negative feelings concerning a situation the Responding Partner is unhappy about. This can get frustrating for the Searcher and push the

Searcher toward their own Protect Mode. We may try to be patient, but we all have our limits.

We can deal with this problem by looking for **Turning Points**. Since half empty glasses are also half full, the Searcher can alter their response to guesses concerning what their partner longs for, rather than dwelling only on what their partner is unhappy about. Exploring these kinds of feelings can help couples move toward making concrete plans for positive change.

We need to spend some time attending those negative feelings first. Our partner needs to feel they have been heard and respected before they will be able to move into more positive directions. Jack might use a Turning Point effectively by saying, "I'm guessing you feel lonely because I only want to talk about football. Perhaps you are wishing I would pay attention to how your day has gone."

Sometimes partners find themselves stuck because of conflicting needs. Perhaps both partners are tired and neither wants to wash the dishes. The first step towards resolution is to reduce emotional pressure by using one's Search Path. Otherwise, each member is apt to push for a solution that sacrifices the needs of the other partner. Once emotional pressure has been reduced and both partners understand each other's feelings and the reasons for them, they can begin to negotiate a solution that meets both of their needs. A good way to start is by brainstorming solutions and looking at those possibilities in the light of meeting the needs of both partners. Options might be to take turns:

Jim agrees to wash dishes this time with the understanding that Frank will make the sacrifice next time that they both are tired. The couple might play "Rock, Paper, Scissors" and leave it to chance. The loser washes. The couple might agree to leave the mess soaking in the sink until morning. Perhaps they decide to do the dishes together and get the job done twice as fast. Many options become available once the couple has reduced emotional pressure enough to work out a solution together.

In any Briar Patch situation, getting off track is not the end of the world. It just means our partner isn't calming down but may be getting more upset. The Searcher can get back on track by putting their own point of view on hold for a while and calmly following the Search Path process:
1) Calm yourself.
2) Guess your partner's feelings and reasons for them.
3) Listen to your partner's response.
4) Adjust your next guess based on this new information.
5) Continue this process until your partner feels fully heard and understood.

As has been stated before, we cannot attend our partners very well while we are trying to give attention to our own perspective at the same time. It is okay to let go of our own mind set for a while. Our ideas will return if they are important. We get better at listening to our partner in a way that calms them when we develop the self-discipline and patience to put our own point of view on hold for the time being. Our chance to have our own emotional pressure reduced will come in time, after we have calmed our partner enough for our partner to be in receptive Connect Mode as well.

Focus Questions for Chapter 4

1) Why is taking time to calm ourselves an important part of our Search Path?

2) Why is it more important to learn to control our own emotional reactions than to attempt to control our partner's?

3) What happens to our upset partner when we calmly attempt to understand their point of view?

4) What are common ways we try to calm our partners that actually may have the opposite effect?

5) It is never too late. If our Protect Mode reactions towards our partner aren't helping, what directive can get things back on track?

What's Next?

We become much more able to stick with our Search Path when we are comfortable using it. In Chapter 5, you will develop confidence that you know how to follow your Search Path and can use the skill easily.

Notes to Myself

Notes to Myself

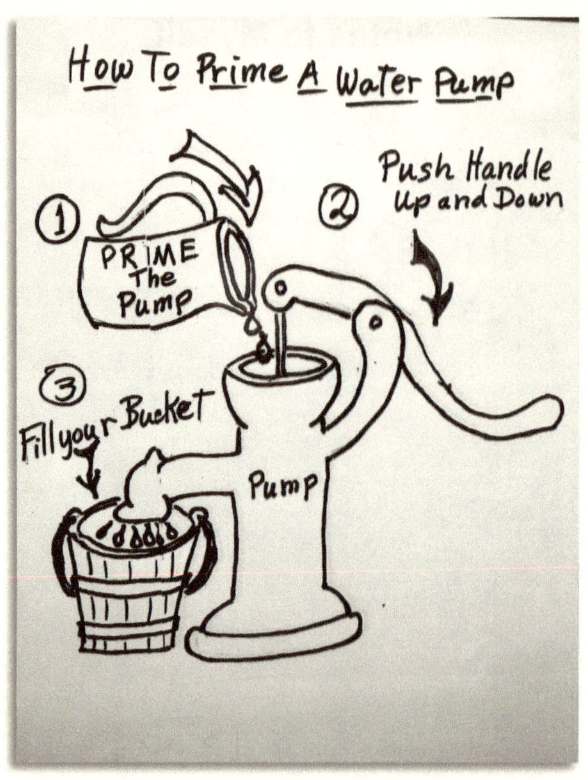

You've got to prime the pump.
You must have faith and believe.
You gotta give of yourself,
'Fore you're worthy to receive.
Drink all the water you can hold.
Wash your face, cool your feet.
Leave a bottle full for others.
Thank you kindly, Desert Pete.

From Desert Pete
By Billy Edd Wheeler 1963

Chapter 5
Search Path Intensive:
Developing Your Skills

It is important to practice Search Path skills in order to develop the brain connections to use them effectively in real-life. When we find ourselves in difficult real-life situations, it is easy for us to get upset and move into our Protect Mode, where we will have difficulty focusing on our partner's perspective rather than our own. However, when we have practiced enough to be comfortable with our Search Path skills, simply being aware that we know what to do will help us calm ourselves. Then we can more easily remain in Connect Mode and use these skills effectively.

Initially, you may find using your Search Path a bit awkward because it is probably not how you usually communicate. So, below is detailed breakdown of the skills involved.

If all this information is overwhelming, the main thing to remember for your Search Path is to:
1) Keep your calm;
2) Guess your partner's feelings and reasons for them;
3) Wait;
4) Guess again based on your partner's response;
5) Continue until your partner feels calm and understood.

When you use these skills to model interest and concern for your partner's feelings, you "Prime the Pump", as "Desert Pete" describes below cartoon at the beginning of this chapter. Then your partner is more likely to reflect your effort and show interest and concern for your feelings in return.

Step #1: Develop Self-Calming Skills

As the Searching partner, you will need to settle into receptive Connect Mode, that calm space within yourself, in order to imagine what your partner's point of view might be. When we are upset, we tend to get caught in Protect Mode and have difficulty getting beyond our own point of view. People have many different ways of calming themselves. You probably know some that work for you. Some people close their eyes a moment and just focus on taking deep, slow breaths. Then they notice where they are carrying tension in their bodies and let it go. Some carry a little memento from some peaceful time which they can hold in times of stress. It can be physical, like a stone, a shell or medallion. I like to carry a small pocket knife with a well-worn blade that was my father's. He took time to show me how to carve a willow whistle with it when I was a child. Its quiet presence helps me remember I have all the time in the world before me. Some people carry a calming saying, verse or thought in their hearts that they can repeat to themselves to find their calm space. Others simply stop and say a little prayer like, "God, please help me calm down and be present here with my partner."

If you don't have a good way to calm yourself, it is a good skill to develop. You will find more detailed help in

Chapter 8: Trouble Shooting, under **Finding Your Peaceful Center**, Page 178, and **Lengthening A Short Fuse**, Page 180. There are self-help books recommended under **Further Reading** at the end of this book. There are also helpful resources online that can help you develop self-calming skills using prayer, meditation, mindfulness, relaxation, self-hypnosis, and yoga.

Step #2: Observe Your Partner

As you settle into your calm space, look for evidence from your partner's concerns and emotional state that can give you a sense about how they might be feeling and a reason they might be feeling that way. Imagine how you might feel if you were in your partner's position. Notice your own feelings. We have these little nerves in our brains called mirror neurons that cause us to react with similar feelings to those of our partner. When we are feeling irritated with our partner, there is a good chance our partner is feeling irritated with us as well.

You can also infer your partner's emotional state from your observations about their appearance and behavior. Some clues to look for include your partner's grooming, breathing rate, facial expression, vehemence, choice of words, gestures, and topic of conversation. Perhaps you notice your partner is red-faced and breathing heavily. Maybe your partner is quiet and seems preoccupied about something. Remember, you don't have to be correct about your guess. It just needs to be based on observations that make sense.

Step #3: Make Your First Guess

Think of a name or label for the feelings you believe your partner might be carrying. Then decide a reason why your partner (or anyone) might feel that way if they were in that situation. State your guess to your partner using the following general format: "I think you might be feeling ________a________ because ______b______." Couch your statement in tentative words that leave your partner room to correct your guess. Rather than saying "I know" you feel ________a________ because ________b________, use terms like "perhaps," or "I think," or "it sounds like," or "maybe." Saying "I know" invites an argument if your partner disagrees. Remember, this is NOT about asking how your partner feels. This approach works through the Searcher making guesses about their partner's feelings, not asking questions.

Keep your guess short and to the point. Then wait. Your purpose is to get your partner talking, not to dominate the conversation yourself. A common mistake is for the Searcher to nervously ramble on. The awkward pause after you make your guess helps focus both partners' attention. Your goal is to get your partner talking so you can help reduce the emotional pressure your partner is carrying, rather than for you to fill all the gaps in the conversation

When you make your guess, maintain eye contact with your partner and use a neutral, enquiring tone of voice. You don't need to sound sugary sweet, and neither do you want to project irritation or impatience. In a way, through your guess, you are asking a question of your partner, which, as has been discussed previously, can be self-defeating by itself. But you are also supplying a possible acceptable answer. This prevents the questioning aspect of your statement from seeming threatening.

Step #4: Listen to Your Partner's Reply

After remaining silent for a time while your partner gathers their thoughts, listen attentively when your partner responds to your guess. Attentive listening is more than just recognizing the noise your partner makes. Listen both for *content* (what your partner is trying to tell you) and *affect* (the emotions that motivate your partner to give you this information). This involves being aware of your partner's whole expression, including body posture and movement, tone of voice, choice of words, facial expression, eye contact, and other physical indications of emotion.

Your partner is likely to respond to your guess in one of two ways:

1) If you are right with your guess, your partner is likely to relax, take a look inside, and agree. Then, if you wait patiently, or encourage your partner by saying "Tell me more," your partner is likely to offer more insight into their point of view and relax still further. In your listening, notice what you got right and any additions your partner offers.

2) If you miss the mark with your guess, which is likely to be the case much of the time, your partner will take pleasure in correcting either one or both parts of your statement. Most human beings love to straighten out someone else's error. In your listening, notice where you missed the mark and what adjustments you will need to make in your next guess.

Step #5: Respond to Your Partner

Before you speak in return after your partner replies to your guess, remember to calm yourself again. Initially, you might try writing down your revised guess about your name for your partner's feelings and the reasons your partner might have them, based on the new information you have just heard. This will help you take time to be thoughtful, clear, and concise, rather than just reacting. You can forget the pencil later, after you get good at this skill. Remember your job as Searcher is to help your partner express themselves and for them to discover for themselves that you care about them, rather than for you to talk or try to convince your partner of anything. Continue using the same format: "It sounds like you feel _________x________ because ________y_______," x being the amended feeling's name - alert for changes in your partner's feelings. As your partner feels heard and emotional pressure reduces, feelings often begin to change. Anger can reduce to hurt. Hurt can move towards acceptance and forgiveness.

On the other hand, your partner's feelings may remain stuck or even intensify if your partner doesn't think you accept their emotions, or they think you misunderstand the reasons for them. When this happens, there is still no need to worry. Hold on to your calm center. This is simply more information to help you with your next guess.

You do not have to match the intensity of your partner's emotional expression. These are your partner's feelings, not yours. All you need to do is use your guesses to attempt to recognize and understand your partner's feelings wherever they may lead.

Be ready to respond to subtle or ambiguous corrections in your partner's response. For example, if your partner says, "That's pretty much right," respond to both sides of the ambivalence by replying something like "Oh, I've got it mostly right, but I'm missing something. Tell me more." Then be ready to listen again. Then make your next guess.

Step #6: Watch For Turning Points

As you continue your Search Path by creating this feedback loop of revised guesses that keep the focus on your partner's point of view, your partner will gain confidence that they are being heard and understood. As a result, they are likely to relax more and more, open up, and share their feelings about whatever topic is on their mind. Your partner senses you are interested in their feelings and, hence, are invested in their life. This dissipates your partner's sense of isolation and builds their confidence in your connection.

Remain alert for **Turning Points.** As your partner begins to relax and emotional pressure lowers, they are likely to move beyond the negative feelings that you have been exploring and begin to focus on what they are longing for to satisfy their needs instead. This is evidence that your partner wants to try a different future with you. When you pay attention to these kinds of hopeful feelings, you are encouraging your partner to imagine a path forward, beyond their present frustrations. As you explore these more positive feelings using your Search Path skills, new directions for your relationship begin to become clear.

Step #7: Decide When to Stop

After a time, check in with your partner to see whether they feel heard and understood. If your partner does not, or is feeling stuck and frustrated, review the **Briars in your Search Path** described previously, beginning on Page 61. These approaches may work fine when your partner is in Connect Mode, but when your partner is feeling vulnerable and in Protect Mode, these commonly used attempts to fix things often make matters worse.

Once your partner is feeling heard and understood, you can switch roles. Now you will have an opportunity to express all those thoughts and feelings which you have been patiently placing on hold in order to take good care of your partner's emotional needs.

Step #8: Switch Roles

In following your Search Path, you worked hard to keep your own opinion out of the conversation, no matter whether you agreed, disagreed, or didn't care. But once you have heard your partner out, and they are feeling calm and settled into Connect Mode, they will be more receptive to hearing your point of view as well.

Now your partner can return the favor, by using their Search Path, starting at Step #1, and do the work of guessing *your* feelings and reasons for them. This is like trading back rubs. As you respond to your partner's Search Path guesses about how you feel and why you feel that way, you get to express whatever reactions you have been holding onto, while your partner gets to practice giving you their undivided attention. In your partner's hands, their Search Path becomes a process through which your partner can explore as much of your emotional world and point of view as you care to share. The nice thing about this side of the equation is that now your partner has the job of containing their reactions while they attend your concerns. You, on the other hand, can talk about whatever is on your mind while your partner tries to help you feel relaxed, heard, and understood.

Once, you feel heard and understood, remember that your partner may have built up some emotional pressure again, since they have had to put their point of view on hold while they listened to yours. So, check back in, using your own Search Path once more, to find out more about their feelings now that they have heard your point of view.

Continue taking turns with this process, remembering that the purpose of these exercises is to reduce emotional pressure between you, to build your sense of connection, and to explore each other's emotional worlds. Thus, when both partners have mastered *Love Work* skills, you will be able to share responsibility for calming each other and meeting each other's needs.

Make Your Search Path Your Own

When you find yourself in a conflict situation with your partner, you are likely to fall back on ineffective Protect Mode habits unless you have practiced your Search Path skills enough to use them easily.

So, here is your opportunity to change your Search Path from an intellectual exercise into a useful reality. Below you will find five situations through which using your Search Path can help you reconnect with your partner. Some situations deal with common daily frictions. Some present issues that are potentially life changing, with which you might need professional counseling help if they were the real thing. In either case, following your Search Path is a good place to start.

Make up conversations with your partner or an interested friend in which you each take a role. Try playing out the situations described even if you think they are unlikely. It is good brain exercise to imagine yourself dealing with unusual situations.

One partner assumes the Protect Mode part of the conversation while the other partner uses their Search Path to help move the conversation into calm productive directions. Then switch Search Path roles so that your partner explores your feelings now that they have expressed theirs.

Write numbers 1-5 on scraps of paper, put them in a pot and take turns drawing. You take the Search Path first for the situation number you draw. Initially, it helps to use paper and pen to help you organize your thoughts during your conversation.

Search Path Practice
Love Work **game for Chapter 5:**

1) Money's tight. You forget a Valentine's card. Your partner goes online and buys a $300 pair of earrings you all clearly can't afford. You find out when paying the credit card bill…

1. State your guess about your partner's

(Feelings) _______________________________________

(Reason for those feelings) _____________________

____

____

2. Wait... Listen to your partner's response…
What did you find out? ___________________________

____

3. Based on this new information, adjust your guess and try again.
(Feelings) _______________________________________

(Reason) ____

____

4. Continue this process until your partner feels understood.

5. Now switch roles so that your partner uses their Search Path to explore how you might be feeling, after having heard their point of view.

2) Your partner has been saying a certain political position is "stupid". You don't think it is stupid at all...

    1. State your guess about your partner's

(Feelings) ___________________________________

(Reason for those feelings) __________________

____

____

    2. Wait... Listen to your partner's response...

What did you find out? _______________________

____

    3. Based on this new information, adjust your guess and try again.

(Feelings) _______________________________

(Reason) _________________________________

____

    4. Continue this process until your partner feels calm and understood.

    5. Now switch roles so that your partner uses their Search Path to explore how you might be feeling in this situation, after having heard their point of view.

3) Your partner comes home from work exhausted and want to zone out in front of the TV. You have been dealing with the baby all day and want them to take over...

1. State your guess about your partner's
(Feelings) _______________________________________

(Reason for those feelings) ____________________________

____

____

2. Wait... Listen to your partner's response...
What did you find out? ____________________________

____

3. Based on this new information, adjust your guess and try again.
(Feelings) ____________________________________

(Reason) _____________________________________

____

____

4. Continue this process until your partner feels calm and understood.

5. Now switch roles so that your partner uses their Search Path to explore how you might be feeling, after having heard their point of view.

4) Your partner has been ranting about the home team's defeat for 15 minutes straight. It feels like they are taking it out on you…

1. State your guess about your partner's
(Feelings) ____

(Reason for those feelings) ____________________

____

____

2. Wait... Listen to your partner's response…
What did you find out? ____________________________

____

3. Based on this new information, adjust your guess and try again.
(Feelings) ____

(Reason) ____

____

____

4. Continue this process until your partner feels calm and understood.

5. Now switch roles so that your partner uses their Search Path to explore how you might be feeling, after having heard their point of view.

5) Your partner has been mentioning a coworker a lot. Your partner just made some critical comments about your weight…

1. State your guess about your partner's

(Feelings) ___________________________________

(Reason for those feelings) ___________________

____

____

2. Wait... Listen to your partner's response…

What did you find out? _______________________

____

3. Based on this new information, adjust your guess and try again.
(Feelings) _________________________________

(Reason) __________________________________

____

____

4. Continue this process until your partner feels heard and understood.

5. Now switch roles so that your partner uses their Search Path to explore how you might be feeling, after having heard their point of view.

Increase Your Self Awareness

After practicing these exercises, answer the following questions, then discuss your answers with your partner. They will help each of you build self-awareness of old, communication habits and encourage new, more effective ones.

How did your partner's feelings change as you used your Search Path?

____

____

____

How did that change your feelings?

____

____

Were you aware of points when you or your partner switched from Connect Mode to Protect Mode or vice versa? When?

____

____

____

How did the level of emotional pressure you experienced change depending on which mode your partner was operating in?

____

____

Focus Questions for Chapter 5

1) Why is it important to take a breath and relax in order to follow your Search Path effectively?

2) What observations about your partner can help you make a reasonable guess about their feelings?

3) What are the parts of an effective Search Path guess?
    How is your partner likely to respond if you guess correctly?
    How is your partner likely to respond if you guess wrong?

4) On what do you base your follow up Search Path guesses?

5) What are Turning Points? How can you use them in your Search Path?

What's Next?

Up until now you and your partner have changed roles between Searcher and Responder simply by taking turns. In Chapter 6, you will learn to use your **Share Path** to develop effective ways to get your partner's attention when you would like them to take care of your needs, rather than you always having to take care of theirs.

Notes to Myself

91

Notes to Myself

92

Chapter 6
Your Share Path:
What About Me? I've Got Feelings Too!

In Chapters 3 through 5, we looked at ways to calm and connect with our partners by using Search Path skills. This works nicely when our partner carries the load of emotional pressure in the relationship while we are relatively pain-free. But how do we get our partner's attention productively when we are the ones carrying the load and when we need our partner to meet *our* emotional needs instead? We can't hold emotional pressure forever. We are only human, and it takes energy to hold back what is on our minds. When our partners begin to relax and talk, we, who are following our Search Path, are likely to find our emotional pressure increasing. We may well have a differing point of view from our partner's, but we can't express it while our partner is doing the talking. When the pressure we carry reaches the breaking point, we will begin to ignore our partner's concerns and switch to our own Protect Mode points of view regardless of our good intentions. When this happens, the old argument cycles are likely to start back up and we will be in danger of losing the connection we have been working so hard to improve.

This is why it's important for both partners to feel heard and understood. Unless the pressure is reduced to the point where neither partner is carrying much emotional load, relationship problems are likely to flare back up. This reduction of emotional pressure depends on both partners' developing the ability to temporarily contain their own Protect Mode reactions while they reduce their partner's emotional pressure. Partners can achieve this balance by trading Search Path roles every so often, so that neither has to contain their own emotional reactions indefinitely.

The best time to trade roles is when one partner is feeling calm and fully heard. This is because the calm partner will be in Connect Mode and will want to make their partner comfortable as well. However, this isn't always possible. Sometimes, the Searching Partner may reach such a high level of frustration that they can no longer listen, even though their partner has not finished expressing their point of view. Sometimes, the time available for the exchange may be running out, and it is unwise to leave one person carrying all the pressure at the conversation's end. Perhaps the Searcher's efforts to understand their partner seem to have reached a dead end for the time being. A period of thought may be needed so that both partners can digest the conversation. Only after reflection will further exploration become possible.

Whatever the reason, how partners go about initiating a switch in roles can make a big difference in their success in finding a calm, reconnected space with each other.

Using our Share Path

When our emotional load is becoming uncomfortably heavy, we can invite a productive change of focus to our own concerns by using our **Share Path**. The Share Path

Your Share Path:

is similar to the Search Path approach that we have already discussed in that it involves naming feelings and the reasons for them. The difference is that now we change our focus to our own feelings and our reasons for those rather than continuing to focus on our partner's feelings.

"Ahhh…", you say, breathing a sigh of relief! "This is what I have been wanting to do all along! Why don't we dispense with this Search Path stuff and get my point of view out on the table?"

Here's why. For our Share Path to work, our partner must be ready to listen. Once we have modeled listening behavior using our Search Path, our partner is more likely to return the favor and listen to us as well. Thus, we will be more likely to get our needs met if we use our Search Path first, before trying our Share Path.

So, assuming you have been using your Search Path to connect with your partner, how do you make the switch so that your partner will begin to accommodate your point of view?

To show how your Share Path works, imagine the following scenario in which your partner makes you uncomfortable. As you read the example, consider how you might use this situation to practice using your Share Path in your own life. For clarity's sake, we will use a concrete example: conflict over a coffee table. In real life situations, the same strategy is useful with any situation in which conflict arises: cleanliness habits; chores; who to invite to dinner; how to handle the kids; getting time and attention; love making; money issues; etc. The list is endless.

So, imagine that you and a friend, Nate, have just decided to become apartment mates. You don't have a formal agreement, but you are hopeful that your relationship will turn into something more. After you both have gotten moved in and he begins to relax, Nate settles back on the couch and props his feet up on your coffee table. Normally this would not bother you, but this happens to be the expensive Chinese heirloom your grandmother left you, which you value highly! Suddenly you find yourself carrying a load of emotional pressure. Your new friendship is out the window. You had been in pleasant Connect Mode, pleased that Nate has joined you in this new adventure. But now Nate has suddenly invaded your space with behavior that threatens your stuff. There is risk that he will scratch your precious table. What do you do? Caught by surprise, you are likely to find yourself descending into Protect Mode. You will be tempted to try protecting your treasure with a fight or flight response.

An example of a fight response might be for you to attempt to force Nate to remove his feet by using a "Push" statement, offering some more or less polite version of, "Get your feet off my coffee table!" An example of a flight response might be to ignore what is happening, or to pretend nothing is wrong while offering a cushion for Nate's feet. Notice where the emotional pressure lies in each of these solutions.

Using the fight response, you may achieve the result you want if you ask Nate to remove his feet from the table. But there is collateral damage. You have shifted the emotional load you are carrying onto Nate. Now you feel fine about your table, but Nate feels criticized and becomes less comfortable and friendly. Emotional distance has been created by his behavior. Your subsequent request doesn't remove the emotional pressure from your relationship. It just shifts it around.

On the other hand, with a flight response, if you ignore Nate's behavior and say nothing in order to avoid awkwardness, then you continue carrying the emotional load instead. You will be glad when Nate leaves and uncomfortable when he returns because you'll worry that Nate's feet will once again threaten your heirloom. The emotional distance will remain as well. Offering the cushion is a gentler flight response solution, but it still implies that Nate has made an unacceptable faux pas. So he may feel embarrassed, but not sure what he has done wrong, and you are likely to feel irritated that you had to put cushions under his feet to protect your possessions. The emotional distance still remains.

The Share Path Advantages

How might this scenario end differently if you had followed your Share Path and said, "Nate, I'm worried about my coffee table. I'm afraid you might scratch it"? Nate would likely respond by removing his feet and apologizing. You would then thank him for his consideration and your relationship would be back on track. With the issue resolved, both of you can return to Connect Mode, the emotional pressure shared and removed.

What made the difference? We experience different reactions when we are told *what to do* rather than being told *how someone feels*. Both approaches may get Nate's feet off the table, but the second method results in connection while the first results in emotional distance.

Pushing someone to do something creates a power struggle and evokes feelings of resistance from the other person. Emotional pressure increases. In contrast, sharing how we feel suggests that we have confidence in our relationship with them. Sharing our feelings and reasons for them tends to build connection and cooperation. Emotional pressure lowers. After you shared your feelings, Nate removed his feet from the table, less because of pressure from you and more out of his own concern for you, in order to make you feel better. You gave the gift of your feelings. Nate gave a gift in return: removing his feet in order to relieve your discomfort.

This works well when, as in this example, someone can accommodate our feelings easily. But that person is under no obligation to do so. Helping you out is their choice, not something they are being required to do. So what happens when we add to the equation a conflict of needs, and accommodating your needs is not in the other person's best interest?

Using the same scenario with Nate's feet on the coffee table, imagine using your new Share Path skill in which you name your own feelings and your reasons for them in order to gain Nate's cooperation. However, this time, rather than removing his feet, Nate explains that he has a blood circulation problem and he might get a blood clot if he doesn't keep his feet up. Now what do you say? You care about your coffee table, but you care about Nate's health too. You might, at that point, try to reach a satisfactory solution for both of your needs by suggesting that you could get a cushion for Nate's feet, or some other option for keeping his feet up while at the same time protecting your coffee table. Problem solving happens more easily when you both are using your Share Paths to express your respective concerns. Not only are both of your needs more likely to get met, but you build a stronger connection as you take care of each other.

Now look at what happens if you don't take time to find your Share Path but use a pushier solution instead. You look over at your new apartment mate lounging with his feet on Grandma's table, and you say, "Please get your feet off my coffee table." You have not shared your feelings, so Nate is likely to feel taken aback and be less likely to share his reasons for needing to use your heirloom as an ottoman. If he obliges your demand, he endangers his health. If he refuses, emotional pressure abruptly increases into confrontation. Until both your needs are understood, there is no basis for negotiation and emotional pressure continues to disrupt your relationship. Creative solutions are much easier to reach when both parties are clear about their feelings and their reasons for them.

It is inevitable at times for us to feel that our partner is oblivious to our needs, just as Nate was oblivious to your feelings concerning your coffee table. These situations can become opportunities to build our relationships when we use our Share Path, communicating how we personally feel and why, rather than just trying to make our partner do something.

The Share Path skill is similar to the Search Path in that it focuses on feelings. However, rather than focusing on our partner's feelings and reasons for them as in the Search Path example which we already practiced (" I guess you are feeling ___________ because ___________"), with the Share Path, we focus on our *own* feelings: "I'm feeling _________ because _________."

Notice that we don't need to couch our own feelings in tentative terms, using phrases such as "I think," or "perhaps," as we would when guessing our partner's point of view. If we have taken time to examine our feelings, then we know what they are. When we express them, we will do the job best if we speak our feelings clearly and unambiguously. For example, if a guy gets way too affectionate way too fast, a girl would do better to say, "I'm uncomfortable with being rushed, because it makes me feel disrespected." Offering a tentative, "I think maybe this isn't okay." leaves the subject open to argument.

Like the Search Path, the Share Path can be a process made up of a number of statements in which a partner can share their point of view while reducing likelihood of triggering a Protect Mode response from their partner. For example, in the coffee table example, what if Nate's response to you sharing your concern had not fully relieved your anxiety. Perhaps he says, "Don't worry, I'll be careful not to scratch it." But you remain anxious that he might. You could escalate with a Protect

Mode push and say, "Just get your feet off my coffee table!" Of course, this will likely create additional emotional pressure and further damage your relationship with Nate. On the other hand, you could use your Share Path again by saying, "I appreciate your willingness to be careful, but accidents happen so I'm still anxious about my table getting damaged." In this way, you make sure Nate realizes his reassurance has not yet met your needs, and that, for you to be comfortable, he will need to do something more.

So now we have two approaches for reducing emotional pressure in our relationships. We can focus on our partner's feelings by using our Search Path to reduce the emotional load our partner is experiencing, or we can focus on expressing our own concerns by using our Share Path if we are carrying an emotional load of which our partner is unaware. Using these tools, either of us can move concerns affecting our relationship to front and center in our conversation in a way than that encourages mutual accommodation and problem solution.

Using Search and Share Path Skills for Real

When you feel ready to try Search Path and Share Path skills in real life situations, begin by dealing with issues that have less emotional impact at first. For example, you might explore each other's outlook on what movie to attend or pizza flavor to choose. Be sure and check in with your partner and see how your efforts leave them feeling. Their reactions will be the best indicator of your skill mastery. As you gain confidence, you can move to tougher problems.

You might try re-examining old arguments you may have had in the past. Notice when each of you fell into Protect Mode. Then talk about ways you could have used your Search and Share Path Skills to move yourselves into Connect Mode.

Finally, when you are feeling brave, try your Search Path with current conflicts. If you find yourselves getting upset, take a break to think some and calm down. Two people in Protect Mode don't accomplish much. But remember to set a time to reconnect and try again. At each stage, as you progress through this gradual increase of emotional intensity, you will find it helpful to return to the **Increase Your Self Awareness** exercises described at the end of Chapters 5 and 6. These will give you feedback help to continue improving your Search Path skills.

Love Work Game for Chapter 6:
Make These Skills Your Own

Below you will find another practice game to play out with your partner or friends. Your Love Work skills are only theoretical until you practice them enough to make them your own.

For each of the 5 situations:

A) Try a **Push** approach, in which you tell your partner what you want him to do. But do it without telling your partner how you are feeling.

How does your partner respond?

B) Try using your **Search Path**. Attend your partner's feelings and reasons for them.

How does your partner respond differently?

C) Try using your **Share Path** to let your partner know that you're are carrying an emotional load using the format, "I'm feeling __________, because __________."

How does your partner respond differently?

1) Your partner agreed to clean the toilets Saturday mornings, but hasn't gotten around to it for a couple of weeks.
A (Push)_______________________________________

____

B (Search)_______________________________________

____

C (Share)_______________________________________

____

2) You think your partner is taking too many pain killers. They don't want to talk about it.
A (Push)_______________________________________

____

B (Search)_______________________________________

____

C (Share)_______________________________________

____

3) Your partner wanted anniversary flowers but is critical of your gift because they "had to ask."

A (Push)____

____

B (Search)____

____

C (Share)____

____

4) Your partner's stuff tends to collect in piles around the house. You like things neat and in order.

A (Push)____

____

B (Search)____

____

C (Share)____

____

5) You have worked hard for three years developing your local business. Your partner just got a great job offer in another country.

A (Push)_________________________________

____

B (Search) _______________________________

____

C (Share) ________________________________

____

Increase Your Self Awareness

What did you notice about the emotional pressure each of you carried as you tried out each role?

____

____

What happened to the overall level of emotional pressure between you as you tried each strategy?

____

____

Which strategies led to better problem resolution? Why?

____

____

Your Share Path:

Focus Questions for Chapter 6

1) Both Share Path and Search Path techniques describe feelings and reasons for them. How are they different?

2) When your partner is in Protect Mode, which Path should you use first? Why?

3) Why is using your Share Path often more effective than just telling your partner what you want them to do?

4), How can you get conflicting concerns out in the open so you can work towards mutual accommodation?

What's Next?

At this point, *Love Work* has provided effective ways to lower the emotional pressure between you and your partner, enabling you to reconnect as partners rather than as adversaries. This helps you live in a comfortable, mutually respectful relationship in which power is shared.

But how can you as a couple manage to get tasks accomplished without ramping the emotional pressure back up again? Someone needs to make decisions. Someone needs to accommodate and help out with those decisions. Sometimes you may feel strongly enough about something to want that decision to be yours, while your partner may have other ideas.

Some approaches work better than others when you are trying to get things done. In Chapter 7, we will look at options for getting beyond making good connections with your partner and on towards working together to set goals and achieve daily tasks.

Your Share Path:

Notes to Myself

It's a Matter of Perspective
I've got this guy trained to give me food!

Chapter 7
Your Action Path:
Getting Your Partner's Cooperation

If you have been practicing the skills presented so far, you have begun to develop skills to reduce emotional pressure between you and your partner. As a couple, you have learned two ways to understand each other more deeply and have created a sense of yourselves as a team. A sign of your success will be that you will begin living in the pleasant kingdom of We-dom. You will find yourselves saying "We're" doing this or "We're" planning that. You and your partner will have become fully integrated into each other's lives.

However, even though you have become experts at using *Love Work* connection skills, your partner is still an individual, separate from you, and is likely to have some goals, plans, and ideas that are different from yours. There will be times when you need your partner's help with things that are important to you. But what if you find your interests are in conflict with things that are important to your partner? How can you, as a couple, handle such situations without damaging your hard earned We-dom?

There are a variety of ways people try to get their partner's cooperation when they have a conflict of interest. Each approach has advantages, and each has some problems associated with it. Each has its place, depending on the circumstances. To help you become aware of your options for managing your differences while still gaining your partner's cooperation, here are a series of stories that demonstrate the ways you might attempt to influence your partner's behavior, together with the likely outcomes for using each strategy. In *Love Work* we call these strategies our **Action Path.** People use all of these approaches, but some work better than others depending on the situation we face. Relationships often founder not because a person thinks they have a problem, but because they think their partner is causing them problems. So how can we manage situations in which someone else is causing the problem? This "Rat Story" evolved over years of experience helping couples learn to work together. The story is based on a series of experiments with little white rats. You will see that there are parallels in human experience.

The Rat Story

Once, in an undergraduate psychology class I was taking, my professor reached into a cardboard box on his desk and pulled out a squirming white rat.

Said he: "For the next three weeks, a rat like this is going to be your teacher."

Thought we: "This guy is nuts!"

Said he: "And the reason it is going to be your teacher is because it acts so much like people."

Thought we: "This guy is really nuts. He has been playing with rats way too long!"

Said he: "And the reason this rat seems so much like people is that 1) he won't listen to anything you have to say, 2) he has a short attention span except for what he's interested in, and 3) he only wants to do what he pleases."

I had to admit, after thinking about the people I've dealt with and how I react myself, that we often operate pretty much the same way as the rat.

Our teacher gave every two students a cardboard box and a cute little rat. He also gave us a popsicle stick, which we were to place into a slot cut near the bottom of the box where the rat could easily reach it.

Our assignment was simple: "Get the rat to push the stick." We were not told how to make this happen. There were five ways students solved this problem. All of them are similar to approaches we use with people, including our partners, to get action. There are advantages and disadvantages to each and informed decisions that we need to make about which we would prefer to use… and have used on us. There is also a sixth approach we use with people that doesn't work with rats, which we will discuss as well.

Getting Your Partner's Cooperation
Through Bribe, Push, or Punish

You are likely to have negative feelings about aspects of the first three of those six strategies. You may feel sorry for the rat, and you wouldn't want them used on you. Ironically, we often use these Bribe, Push, or Punish tactics on our partners without being conscious of what we are doing. Because we don't have to think much about how to do them, they tend to be our first choices when we are in Protect Mode. While these may get the job done, used frequently, they are likely to increase emotional pressure and create distance in place of our hard won We-dom.

Bribe

We first tried to get our rat's cooperation with the **Bribe** technique. We simply smeared a little peanut butter on the stick. We figured our rat would eat the peanut butter and, in the process, push the stick. In fact, our rat did no such thing. Instead, he sat quietly in a corner of the box and proceeded to go to sleep. I took our rat back to the teacher, saying, "Something is wrong with this rat. It won't even eat peanut butter. We need a better rat."

Said he: "You've got a pretty fat looking rat there. Are you sure he is hungry?"

Actually, we had been anxious that the little fellow might die on us, so we had kept him stuffed with all his stomach could hold. So, we put him back in his cage and did not feed him for a day. Then back in the box he went, with peanut butter back on the stick. What happened? The little guy had a whole new personality. He quickly found the stick and gobbled down the peanut butter. We called our teacher over and pointed out that our rat was pushing the stick as he finished his peanut butter.

Our teacher wasn't terribly impressed. He admitted our rat happened to touch the stick as he ate the peanut butter, but said that, since his assignment had said nothing about peanut butter, he would only give us credit if our rat continued to push the stick when we replaced the stick with one that was peanut butter free. We hoped our rat would continue to go to the stick. But no, the rat was not interested in the stick unless peanut butter was involved.

What is the first lesson our rat taught us? If rats aren't hungry, they won't do anything. This rule also applies over a broad range of human situations, as can be seen in the following examples.

A complaining mother comes for counseling with her problem teenager in tow. He is decorated with the latest and most expensive of everything his heart could desire: smart phones, computer tablets, gold chains, tattoos, piercings, the works.

Says mom: "I don't understand it. I'm working three jobs to keep him happy. I give him everything. He won't do his schoolwork. All he does is whine and complain. Please help!" In the meantime, the kid slouches in the chair, ignores the therapist and his mom, and plays with a video game. What does the therapist think? Fat Rat! The boy has been given everything, so he wants nothing. As a result, he has zero motivation to help his mother or do anything to take care of himself. Like the well-fed rat, he is unaffected by any expectation others might have of him. Bribes don't work when the person doing the bribing has nothing more to offer. The solution, of course, is to make the boy hungry. To get what she wants, his mother will need to stop giving him all that he wants for a while. This will be hard for her, for reasons we will get to shortly.

What did we learn from our rat about bribing that the boy's mom needs to learn? 1) It works only when the rat is hungry for the bribe. 2) Once the bribe disappears, the rat's motivation to cooperate disappears also.

I recently found myself the victim of this second problem with the Bribe technique. A painter offered to paint our tin roof at a bargain rate. But before the job was finished, he told me apologetically that he needed a little extra cash. He seemed like such a nice guy, we gave him the rest of the money up front. Suddenly we had trouble getting him to finish painting the roof. Other jobs had become more important to him. There was no more peanut butter on our stick.

These two problems with the Bribe technique happen between partners as well. If Erin frequently over-accommodates David, Erin is likely to find herself complaining, as did the Fat Rat boy's mother, that she does everything for David and he never seems to notice how hard she tries. Because Erin meets all of David's needs and expectations without standing up for her own needs, David takes Erin's efforts for granted. He is not hungry, so he doesn't notice what she does for him. Erin tries to do everything for David out of the mistaken belief that showing her partner such all-giving love will cause David to return the same favor. However, because she meets David's needs before he even knows he has them, Erin ceases to exist in David's awareness in the same way that we don't notice the contribution our refrigerator offers us. We don't love our refrigerator. We just use it. David winds up feeling entitled, lonely, and discontent. Erin winds up feeling unappreciated and resentful. Emotional pressure between them grows. In this way, overuse of the Bribe technique can damage or destroy relationships.

The Bribe technique is often seen in "enabling behavior" as couples attempt to deal with addiction issues. The addicted member keeps asking the enabling member to cover for him one more time. If she does, he promises he will kick the habit and get on the straight and narrow. The enabling member loves her addicted spouse and doesn't want to lose him or see him in trouble, so she puts a little more peanut butter on the stick by covering for him one more time. She calls his boss and tells him she had been sick again and needed her husband's help getting to the doctor. That is why he missed work Monday. But the addict is motivated by his need to get her to cover for him, not by stopping his addictive behavior. So as soon as he gets the peanut butter of her rescue, he collapses back into his addiction. How are they feeling? The addicted member feels anxious, guilty, and manipulative. The enabling member feels betrayed, manipulated, and resentful. Emotional pressure remains high, and their relationship remains caught in a permanent state of crisis. She remains stuck, almost ready to leave. He remains stuck, almost ready to quit his addiction.

Are there times when the Bribe technique is useful? If the rat is hungry, a bribe does lure him to the vicinity of the stick. But the bribe needs to be used sparingly or the rat will no longer be hungry. The free sample at the grocery store is an example of the Bribe technique at work.

With couples, Erin might create the bribe of a great meal to lure David home from the pub. And it might work… except that David may well start drinking again after dinner. Dinner is gone. There is no more peanut butter on that stick.

So the Bribe technique is useful for encouraging our partner in directions we desire, but it isn't self-sustaining. We need something more for our partner to become invested in goals we desire, rather than just being interested in short-term rewards.

When people get frustrated with lack of progress using bribes, they often resort to force, thinking that perhaps they can make their partner do what they want. Attempts at using force can come in a vast number of guises: hinting, asking, begging, threatening, demanding, nagging, and guilting, to name a few. This brings us to the Push technique. We looked at using a Push briefly in Chapter 6 as a less effective option to using one's Share Path.

Push

In our Rat Story, a fellow student, Ben, tried a simple, direct idea. He grabbed his rat behind the head and pushed the rat onto the stick. The rat had to push the stick. He had no other choice. Ben called the teacher over, made his rat push the stick, and asked for his "A" grade.

The teacher admitted that the rat was pushing the stick but pointed out that the rat wasn't doing the job on his own. He suggested that Ben was actually pushing the stick and the rat was simply caught in the middle. He suggested that Ben find out what would happen if he stopped pushing. So, Ben shoved the rat onto the stick about 20 times to make sure that it got the idea and then sat back and waited without pushing the rat further. What did the rat do? Whatever he pleased, and that usually did not include pushing the stick.

Here's a human application of the Push technique: Jim is watching TV, ignoring his wife, Liz. She wants him to get a job as he had promised.

Liz starts pushing: "Why don't you go out and get a job? Jim, you need to make some calls! How many times do I have to ask you to do your share? I'm working three jobs. How come you can't find one? Why don't you ever take responsibility? Your brother has got a great job. You ought to be like him! It's your family duty to get working! I'm very disappointed in you! You're not going to see the end of trouble until you get yourself moving!" This barrage continues indefinitely, while Jim grunts occasionally and ignores her.

Eventually if she demands, questions, whines, nags, threatens, and complains long enough, Jim will stop grunting and instead snarl, "All right, I'll go get a job! Tomorrow… Now GET OFF MY CASE!" The next day Big Jim does a poor job of getting one by enquiring half-heartedly at a few places. Then he settles back down in front of the TV.

What happened here to Liz? She got her way, kind of, but she also got bitten: treated disrespectfully by her irritated husband. In the Rat Story, Ben managed to avoid getting bitten by carefully holding his rat behind the head when he tried his pushing experiment. It is hard to hold an irritated spouse behind the head. Nobody enjoys getting pushed very much, and those who get pushed a lot often react negatively by biting or pushing back in response.

Now what is going to happen tomorrow with Liz and Jim? You guessed it. Jim will continue to do nothing unless Liz continues her thankless task of pushing him to get a job. In fact, since people get used to all this pushing and nagging after a while, Liz will have to push harder and longer to get Jim's half-hearted response along with his biting negative reaction. What is more likely to happen is that Liz will get tired of pushing and take on additional work herself to cover the bills. In either case, whether she is pushing Jim or doing extra work, Liz continues to carry the whole load. Jim isn't engaged or motivated. Pushing does not create motivation.

So, are there times when the **Push** technique is useful? A polite push works fine when there is no emotional pressure in the way. It is a direct way to communicate our desires when the person being pushed is happy to help. For instance, "Pass the salt, please" is a gentle push. Pushing also works in emergencies. If our partner doesn't see a stop light and is about to drive into crossing traffic, it is important that we push by screaming "STOP!" It is also one of the few techniques available to get at least some compliance from an unmotivated Fat Rat (or person) who isn't hungry for anything we have to offer. However, when we over-rely on the Push technique, we will have to keep creating a sense of emergency in order to keep up the intensity needed to keep our partner moving. This gets tiring and irritating for everyone involved.

We can tell when we are part of a couple relationship that is overusing the **Push** technique when we start noticing resistance to our efforts. One partner may begin to hear these kinds of complaints: "You never listen to me. You are like talking to a brick wall." Or from the other partner, "You nag me to death!" How do we feel as a couple when we are caught in this pattern? One partner is feeling ignored. The other is feeling pushed around. Neither feels loved. As a result, emotional pressure is high and there is a great deal of resistance in the relationship with little energy left to get things accomplished.

Often people get caught in this cycle because they have never learned other options. Perhaps they grew up in a family that lived in a constant state of emergency and pushing was the only way that they thought they could survive. There are more comfortable options available, which we will discuss shortly. But first we need to look at a transformation of the Push technique which occurs when the couple's frustration reaches the breaking point. Then they move beyond Push to Punish.

Punish

In our Rat Story, Jeff, another student, glued copper wire to the bottom of his box to which he hitched an electric shocker. Jeff turned it on and dropped his rat in the box. The shocked rat jumped and ran around in the box. When the frightened rat happened to hit the stick,

Jeff turned off the shocker. After Jeff had repeated this process two or three times, the rat would make a beeline for the stick whenever Jeff put the rat in the box. In *Love Work* we call this the **Punish** technique. Psychologists call it negative reinforcement. Jeff called the teacher over and asked for his "A." The teacher was forbearing and didn't call the SPCA. He did note, however, that the rat wasn't pushing the stick, he was sitting on it. The teacher asked Jeff to predict what would happen if he put the rat in the box with the shocker turned off.

In this situation, it is hard to predict what might happen, since the outcome depends both on the strength of the shock and the personality of the rat. If the shock is mild, or the rat has a laid-back attitude, he might just do what he pleases until he gets shocked. Only then, would he run to the stick. On the other hand, if the shock were severe, or if the rat happened to have a nervous, uptight personality, he might just sit on the stick, afraid to move. So, the only thing we know for sure is that the rat will go to the stick when shocked, and the shocker must stay ready to punish to get their desired result.

Using this approach with people may not suit your personality unless you enjoy being mean or have a need to gain power over others. However, when we move into Protect Mode with our partners, we often find ourselves doing things we don't enjoy. An insecure spouse can move beyond being over controlling -a Push technique- and become abusive and possibly life threatening -a Punish technique- if they fear their subjugated partner is planning their escape. Perhaps Curtis, the guy with the squirrel rifle described in Chapter 3, didn't miss. Maybe he actually was aiming at Ruby and hit his target. He just said he was shooting at the guy who was paying Ruby too much attention. He didn't injure Ruby fatally, and she certainly did not cause him any more trouble thereafter. Partner murder/ suicides that periodically make headlines are examples of extreme Punish technique gone awry.

Usually punishment in couple relationships is much less dramatic. It doesn't have to include violence, screaming, and yelling. When anger is suppressed and emotional pressure is high, common Punish techniques we use include sarcasm, complaining, blaming, and threatening. They also can include acting out behavior, such as giving one's partner the silent treatment, breaking things, or having an affair.

With the Punish technique, the plan is simple: if your partner doesn't do what you want, punish them until they do. Your partner has the option of submission, fighting back, or escaping the relationship. Relationships that rely on this approach tend to be irritating, energy draining, and emotionally toxic. Emotional pressure stays high.

Unlike the rat example, in which the student is safely outside the box and only the rat can get shocked, with couples, if one person shocks the other, the person who has been shocked can return the insult and shock their partner right back. So, in our human relationships, each partner lives in a separate but similar box in relation to their partner. Our partner can return behavior they receive, positive or negative. Couples in our western society can officially leave their box, if things get sufficiently uncomfortable, through divorce. However, it is more difficult to leave the box emotionally. Often the punishment patterns continue long after divorce, as angry former couples continue to find ways to punish each other through fights and legal battles over things like money, property, and children.

Does this mean the Punish technique is always a bad idea? No. Used occasionally and gently when the behavior first begins, it can be very useful to set limits on unacceptable behavior. For example, if your partner seems to have lost their head and acts overly attracted to someone at a gathering, it might be worth your while to take your partner aside and explain your discomfort. Then, ask them to introduce you and acknowledge you as their partner. Popping your partner's balloon is a mild punishment, but it can help keep your relationship primary.

Getting Your Partner's Cooperation Through Reward, Push/ Reward, or Modeling

There are gentler, connection-oriented approaches with which we can influence our partner's behavior, rather than relying on the punitive attempts to force behavior that Punish or Push techniques offer. However, these other approaches require more self-control and forethought. So they work best when we are in Connect Mode. They tend to keep emotional tension low and cooperation levels high.

Your Action Path:

While tactics that increase emotional pressure get a lot of public attention in emergencies, wars, and politics, they are unhealthy, uncomfortable, and energy draining when we have to live with them all the time. Home, at least, should be a place where we can relax and renew our strength. Fortunately, with a little forethought, there are gentle approaches that can get our partner's cooperation. Let's look at Reward, Push/ Reward, and Modeling paths to get the action we desire from our partners while keeping emotional pressure low.

Reward

Returning to our Rat Story, one student was careful not to feed his rat the morning before he placed it in the training box. The hungry rat wandered around for a while and happened, by chance, to bump the stick. At that point, the student dropped a small piece of rat food into the box, which the rat quickly ate. The rat wandered some more and eventually touched the stick again. Again, the student rewarded the rat. The rat found the stick more quickly next time. Before long, the rat would go directly to the stick, poke it, and look expectantly up at his student for his reward. The rat seemed to recognize the deal: "I push the stick; you give me some food." This approach is similar to Bribe, with one important difference. With Reward, the food comes *after* the desired behavior occurs, rather than before.

What did the teacher say when the student demonstrated his rat's prowess? The student got his "A" without argument. Everyone wins with the Reward technique.

Elementary school teachers often use this technique with their students. They call it "Catching Them Being Good." Rather than scolding a student's misbehavior, the teacher makes a point of noticing when the student is showing a behavior the teacher desires. She might say, "Liam, I noticed you shared your crayons with Olivia! That was so kind of you." Then she puts a gold star by his name on the school blackboard. Liam likes the positive attention he gets from this teacher and begins sharing more often. This works for couples too. When we notice and appreciate the special things that our partners do for us, our partners become likely to do more of those special things.

There are some difficulties with this approach. First, returning to our Rat Story model, the rat has to be hungry for what the student has to offer. It doesn't do much good for the student to say, "Good Boy!" to the rat when it happens to push the stick. Rats are motivated by food, not compliments.

With couples, it is useful to have a conversation with our partner to learn what they find rewarding. We may be surprised. For example, many people find compliments embarrassing rather than rewarding. Other rewards may be things which our partner may desire, but which we may feel uncomfortable giving—a cake for a diabetic, for example. It is important to take time to negotiate what is rewarding for one partner and also not a problem for the other. Perhaps the diabetic would go for a backrub instead of the cake.

Your Action Path:

A second difficulty is that emotional pressure must be low for the Reward technique to work well. If we are angry with each other, we might prefer to find something our partner is doing that we can punish, and our partner may not appreciate our reward if we do give one.

A final drawback is that the desired behavior has to occur before it can be rewarded. In the **Push** example Liz is going to have to wait an awfully long time to reward Big Jim for getting a job. He doesn't like working. What if the behavior we wish to reward never occurs? *Love Work* has an answer, for which we will return once more to our Rat Story.

Push/Reward

In the Rat Story, Amanda, another student, first made sure her rat was hungry and then pushed her rat onto the stick as previously described in the Push technique? But, this time, she rewarded it with a little food each time she forced it to touch the stick. The rat might not have been interested in the stick initially, but it quickly came to associate the stick with getting fed. Soon, Amanda could put the rat in the box without pushing it onto the stick and the hungry rat would go check out the stick. When Amanda then rewarded the rat when it touched the stick, the rat quickly learned to touch the stick to get food on its own. Push is not the only thing that can initiate such behavior. Bribe can work as well. Amanda could have put a tiny amount of peanut butter on the stick to interest the rat in that direction. Then, after the rat happened to nudge the stick while looking for a little more, she could Reward him for touching the stick on his own with additional food. Let's call the approach Push/Reward for simplicity's sake. You may remember Grandma's Rule: "As soon as you finish your spinach, we can have dessert." This is an example of Push/Reward. The Push is "eat your spinach", the Reward, fresh strawberry cheesecake. Using the Punishment technique can be problematic as the behavior initiator when using Push/Reward because it may upset the rat to the point that it won't want to eat. People are the same. Excessive punishment may create so much emotional pressure that nothing will serve as an adequate reward. Then, Wicked Stepmother's Rule becomes an issue. Wicked Stepmother and Lucas dislike each other, and emotional pressure is high, so all their interactions feel like punishment. Lucas punishes Wicked Stepmother by not eating spinach. She punishes Lucas by not giving him dessert.

The Push/Reward technique is the way school classes often work: The teacher says, "Read Chapter 24 and do Problems 1, 5, and 7. If you get them right, you get to go to recess early." The "Push" is read the chapter and do the problems. The "Reward" is early recess.

So, while the Push/Reward approach isn't romantic, it is practical. In love relationships, if you can tell your partner what you need and then reward your partner for accommodating that need, your partner is likely to do more of the same in the future. For instance, if you would like your partner to give you flowers for Valentine's Day, but he usually just gives you a card, you would be wise to tell him you would like flowers. While the first year, it won't seem very romantic because you had to tell him, if you reward him by recognizing his efforts and thanking him, he is more likely to volunteer future flowers without your reminder.

Modeling

There is also one other, sixth approach we call **Modeling**, that won't work with rats. But it often works well with people because it relies on our human need for connection and cooperation. Human beings tend to copy the behaviors of those with whom we are emotionally connected. We smile at our babies and get smiles in return. We clean our homes and our children want to help. We build a backyard picnic table and our child wants to hammer on a piece of wood. Likewise, when we listen to a partner using our Search Path, we invite listening in return.

The danger of Modeling is that our negative behaviors get copied too. If our partner grew up getting yelled at, we are likely to get an ear full as well. If we are critical of others, we are likely to get the same behavior reflected back on us. On the other hand, when we take charge of our actions and project a model of behavior that is calm and respectful, even in the face of provocation, we are likely to get the same from our partners in return. "Do unto others as you would have them do unto you" really does work as a recipe for peaceful existence with our neighbors and our partners.

Practice Using Your Action Path

Below is a problem couples may have to deal with. Try out your six Action Path techniques with your partner. Notice how each leaves you and your partner feeling.

 Frequently, your partner promises to help later, then doesn't get around to it... You would like them to keep their promises.

1) Try Bribe: _______________________________

____

____

____

Your Feelings? _______________________________
Your Partner's? _______________________________

2) Try Push: _______________________________

____

____

____

Your Feelings? _______________________________
Your Partner's? _______________________________

Your Action Path:

3) Try Punish: ___________________________________

____

____

____

Your Feelings? _____________________________________

Your Partner's? ____________________________________

4) Try Reward: __________________________________

____

____

Your Feelings? _____________________________________

Your Partners? _____________________________________

5) Try Push/Reward: _____________________________

____

____

Your Feelings? _____________________________________

Your Partners? _____________________________________

6) Try Model: ___________________________________

____

____

Your Feelings? _____________________________________

Your Partners? _____________________________________

Focus Questions for Chapter 7

1) How is using a Bribe to get your partner motivated similar to using a Reward? How is it different?

2) Why should Bribe, Push and Punish techniques be used sparingly?

3) How can we use Reward to make Bribe, Push or Punish techniques more effective?

4) When we Model listening carefully and respectfully to our partner, how is our partner likely to treat us in return?

What's Next?

Action Path techniques help us get things done with our partner. But we need to be fully aware of the emotional impacts of our Action Path, or the Law of Unintended Consequences may rear its ugly head. Chapter 8 will look in more detail at our Action Path in relation to our feelings.

Your Action Path:

Notes to Myself

Notes to Myself

134

Chapter 8
Emotions and Your Action Path

Now that you understand the six ways we can change our partner's behavior, applying them should be straightforward, right? Well, not quite. To change our behavior, we must rewire our brains to operate in new ways. This happens through our close emotional connection with our partner. So, let us look at the role emotions play in how our Action Path works.

Dumping Bad Habits

How can we get rid of our own or our partner's bad habits? Returning again to our Rat Story, after we had taught our rats to push their sticks, our teacher gave us a final task: "Get your rat to *stop* pushing the stick." So here was the next challenge: How can we get rats, our partners, or ourselves to abandon habits that cause us problems? I thought I could stop my rat's stick pushing behavior by ceasing to give him a reward when he pushed the stick. With no reward, I figured the behavior would stop too. What actually happened? To my surprise, the rat began pushing the stick *more*! What happens when we humans are used to putting our dollar in a drink machine, but it refuses to give us our drink when we push the button? Most people don't just shrug and walk away. Instead we keep punching buttons, shake the machine, or reach up inside trying to get it to respond. Emotional inertia can keep us attempting old habits long after they have stopped working. Rats have similar reactions.

After my rat had faithfully pushed the stick numerous times without getting a reward, I began to feel a bit sorry for the little guy. Finally, I couldn't resist giving it a little treat. What did the rat learn? You get rewarded if you push the stick a bunch of times! The rat ended up learning to push the stick more frequently rather than less. This intermittent reinforcement is what keeps people coming back to slot machines in Las Vegas. Even though people pay vastly more into the slot machines than they get back in return, the occasional payback is enough reward to keep them playing. This is why gambling addiction can be such a hard habit to break. This is also why a person may stay in an unrewarding relationship. Every once in a while, something good happens. They keep hoping things will get better.

To stop his rat's behavior, Jeff, the student who had used the Punish technique, glued a wire to the popsicle stick and shocked the rat whenever the rat touched it. This negative reinforcement worked as long as the shocker was turned on, but the rat soon returned to his old habits after the punishment ceased. In another couple relationship example, Amber and Steve grew up in families in which **Punish** was the usual strategy for getting things done. So, they find themselves habitually punishing each other, even though they love each other and want to stop being mean. How can they break that bad habit? They may try hard to practice being nice to each other. But then things don't get done and frustration levels rise until one or the other starts punishing again. When that gets results, punishment has been rewarded once again and the unhappy behavior pattern continues.

There is a way out of this predicament. In the Rat Story, what worked best to discourage the undesirable behavior was, as discussed above, to stop rewarding the undesirable stick pushing behavior. At the same time, the student had at ready a reward to give the rat when it happened to try something else rather than push the stick. When the rat temporarily stopped pushing the stick and wandered to the corner of the box, Amanda gave the rat a food reward in that new location. At that Turning Point, rewarding the new behavior began to become effective.

People work the same way. We have a difficult time being successful at "not doing" bad habits we have developed because we are still focused on the bad habit. We can, however, learn alternative habits that conflict with the one we'd like to stop by focusing on those new habits and rewarding them instead. For instance, rather than eating a bag of potato chips when we get anxious, we could reward ourselves with a crisp apple after going jogging for fifteen minutes. The jog decreases our anxiety and the apple rewards the jog. We are rewarded as well by feeling good about improving our health. As a result, our compulsion to anxiously eat potato chips is likely to decrease.

In the same vein, a couple might wish to stop spending so much time looking at their smart phones, since it leaves them feeling tired and frustrated. So, they decide to use their *Love Work* skills to explore areas of social concern that they would like to address together. As a result, they begin to feel connected with each other rather than alone and swallowed by their smart phones. Because they are rewarded by their new behavior, they become a politically active team rather than passive individual smart phone observers.

Where Do Emotions Fit in the Action Path?

Now you have become aware of the six approaches you are likely to use to get your partner to respond to your need for action: Bribe, Push, Punish, Reward, Push/Reward, and Modeling. So, let's take a look at where emotional pressure rests, if there is any, with each of these strategies. We will return again to our Rat Story model, and then give examples in human relationships.

With the Bribe technique in the Rat Story, the student carries the emotional load. The rat has no problem. He just takes what peanut butter he can get. The student has to keep on investing more and more peanut butter to get the rat to act. The rat stops acting whenever the peanut butter ceases. Codependent human relationships work the same way. The enabling partner carries the emotional load for the addicted person, whose constant plea is, "Just help me out one more time, then I'll straighten up." However, once the enabling partner has again helped the addict out, the addict no longer is motivated to keep their promise.

With the Push technique in the Rat Story, both the student and the rat find their emotional pressure increasing. The student's load increases because he has to invest energy in getting the rat to do what he would like it to do. The rat's load increases as well, because the rat is being forced to do something other than what it would like to do. In human societies, this is the reason why tyrannies are unstable. Remember the saying, "Uneasy rests the head that wears the crown." This remains true whether the tyrant is a dictator or a nagging spouse.

Another expression, "Where there is a will, there is a way!" may work for self-discipline. But for couples, a more accurate expression is, "Where there is a *will*, there is a *won't!*" We each like to be in charge of our own life. So, the more we push our partners, the more resistance, frustration, and emotional pressure we are likely to receive in return. When emotional pressure from excessive use of the Push technique becomes intolerable, Push evolves into Punish, setting the stage for painful levels of emotional pressure, revolt, or divorce.

With the Punish technique in the Rat Story, both the student and the rat find their emotional loads rapidly escalating. The rat's load increases because it is being hurt to force its cooperation. The student's emotional load increases because he either must face a sense of personal guilt in mistreating another living being or he must frame the rat as bad or worthless in order to feel OK about his cruel behavior. Also, the rat may react by punishing the student in return with a nasty bite. In the same way, couples caught in escalating cycles of punishment must endure high levels of emotional pressure and are likely to feel badly about themselves or devalue their partners in order to justify their own poor behavior.

When the Reward technique is used in the Rat Story, emotional pressure decreases both for the student and the rat. The student feels emotional relief because he recognizes that the rat is doing something that he wants. Thus, the student has a greater sense of control. The rat feels relief too, both because it is being rewarded and because it gets a greater sense of control as well. It knows what it can do to get fed. Likewise, when couples make a habit of rewarding each other frequently, they experience similar emotional pressure relief. They also create long-term relationship stability and satisfaction as they learn more and more how to please each other.

With the Push/ Reward technique, the student and the rat both carry an initial emotional load as described above under Push. However, once the rat has responded to the push and gotten rewarded by the satisfied student, the emotional pressure for both is reduced. In the same way, couples do well when they are clear with each other about their needs (the popsicle stick in the Rat Story) and make a habit of rewarding their partner's help in meeting those needs (the food reward in the Rat Story).

With couples, the Push/ Reward approach shows a realistic understanding of human limitations and willingness to work together within these limitations. An important limitation is that we aren't very good at reading each other's minds most of the time. So, we will do well to clearly let our partner know what we need, and then reward our partner when they attempt to meet that need.

Our emotional pressure may build initially, since we have to expose ourselves to possible rejection when we express our needs. Also, our partner is likely to experience an initial increase in emotional pressure, since they will have to stop what they were focusing on in order to attend to us. However, as we try to accommodate our partner and reward our partner's efforts to accommodate us, we will both develop confidence that accepting a Push will lead to Reward.

So emotional pressure increases initially for the rat when we try to eliminate unwanted behavior by withholding reward or using mild punishment. However, emotional pressure quickly reduces once the rat discovers a new behavior that gets rewarded instead. This approach works fine for people as well, so long as the new behavior is rewarded and the punishment for the undesirable behavior is acceptable for both partners.

If the punishment is deemed unfair, or one's partner is not interested in developing the new behavior, emotional pressure and resistance to change increases quickly. So, changing behaviors that affect a couple need to be negotiated. Both partners need to agree on the plan, with clear goals for change (the rat's popsicle stick,) and agree on acceptable rewards and punishments.

Withholding reward or using punishment to suppress unwanted behavior without rewarding alternative behavior causes emotional pressure to rapidly increase and may well not get us the alternative behavior we were expecting. For example, our dogs once found a weak spot in our young son's chicken pen and destroyed half his flock. I wired a dead chicken to an electric fence charger and confined the dogs within easy reach of the chicken, while I repaired the chicken pen with strong new fencing. The dogs were very respectful of the electrified chicken, but, once released, they quickly tore through the new wire and killed the rest of our flock. Thus ended our son's egg enterprise. The punishment of a shock had suppressed the dogs' behavior toward the wired chicken. But, since I had not helped the dogs develop new behaviors that were more rewarding than killing chickens, the dogs quickly returned to the undesirable behavior once they were able to do so.

Thus, in changing either our partner's habits or our own, suppressing a behavior we don't like needs to be combined with reward and support for alternative behaviors that we do like. For example, we could agree to suppress habitual arguing behavior with the mild punishment of agreeing to go for a brisk walk to blow off steam when we find ourselves arguing. It is difficult to argue and walk quickly at the same time, and the exercise uses up excess adrenaline. We might also agree that, when we return from our walk, we develop an alternative behavior to arguing by practicing our Search Path skills. Our reward will be reducing the emotional tension we experience and gaining deeper understanding and a stronger emotional connection with our partner.

Hence, Bribe, Push, and Punish techniques may be useful short-term, but there is a cost involved in terms of increased emotional pressure with each. This pressure will have to be dealt with, or our relationship will become increasingly strained and nonfunctional. In contrast, Reward and Push/Reward techniques are more problem-free because they help develop long-term cooperative and mutually beneficial relationships while also reducing emotional pressure.

Modeling works great as a motivator when little emotional pressure is involved. Since our relationship is close, being social creatures, we enjoy copying each other's efforts and working together at a task. For example, if company is coming at six and your partner is scrambling to get ready, you will probably scramble to help as well, rather than sit back and play video games.

However, when our ideas diverge and emotional pressure begins to build, modeling negative behavior is likely to increase. For example, perhaps you didn't want a party, so you are playing video games rather than helping your partner prepare. Your irritated partner begins to nag you. Then you model that behavior by arguing back. When such a situation develops, taking time out to use *Love Work* skills can reduce emotional pressure and allow you to realign your priorities so that modeling can again become an effective tool for cooperation.

Most couples who openly communicate their preferences to each other and seek to accommodate each partner's needs gradually negotiate interaction habits which rely primarily on Reward, Push/Reward, and Modeling approaches. This creates a stable, positive, high-energy environment for their family. There is extra energy available because little energy is wasted dealing with bad feelings or containing high levels of emotional pressure. Instead, that energy is available for learning, enjoying each other, and being creative forces in the world. This state of We-dom is a comfortable, productive place. Bribe, Push, and Punish approaches are best reserved for occasional emergency situations. These will need to be cushioned with Search Path decompression time afterwards to get back on a positive track with low emotional pressure.

Focus Questions for Chapter 8

1) What happens to the emotional pressure between you and your partner when you Bribe, Push, or Punish your partner until they accommodate you?

2) What happens to the emotional pressure between you when you Reward your partner for accommodating your needs?

3) If you and your partner think you argue too much, how can you stop? What good habit would you like to replace that bad habit with? How can you encourage more of that new behavior?

4) Which strategies are best reserved for emergencies? Which strategies work best to create a low-pressure, high-energy living environment for you and your partner?

Emotions and Your Action Path:

Notes to Myself

Notes to Myself

146

Chapter 9
Skill Integration:
Putting It All Together

So far, you have learned sets of skills you can use to create and maintain stable productive relationships. This chapter extends that learning, showing you which situations call for the use of a particular skill and also how to use your skills in combination. You now know, for example, that you can use your Search Path to help reduce the emotional load your partner is carrying. You realize that doing this until your partner feels heard and understood creates a receptive environment for you to express what is on your own mind as well. You also have developed your Share Path skill, both to relieve your own emotional pressure and to direct your partner's attention towards your concerns. Your partner, in turn, can use their Search Path skills to demonstrate concern for your emotional needs. Doing this for each other enables you to connect comfortably and work as a team. Once emotional pressure is reduced, you have available your Action Path skills: the six ways of encouraging actions you would like from your partner.

Both you and your partner can use these strategies to influence how your relationship develops and how your family operates. But whose responsibility is it to begin these efforts when there is a problem? *It is always yours!* You have real control only over your own behavior, not your partner's. If you wait for your partner to take the initiative because you think your partner is responsible for the problem, then you are likely to remain feeling out of control and frustrated. Your partner may not even realize that you are carrying an emotional load, or they may be too anxious and caught up in Protect Mode themselves to remember to use the *Love Work* skills that you have been practicing. When *you* take responsibility for initiating use of these skills, you begin to have a positive influence on how your relationship develops.

Integrating Your Skills

The following story shows how we can use our various skills together in dealing with situations that might arise in our relationships. Life in rural Virginia often involves pickup trucks and antique ways of thinking, but the relationship problems that need to be worked out are universal.

Zach and Mary's First Date

Zach is about to take Mary out on her first date. Before he arrives, Mary's mom tells Mary that a sign that Zach cares for and respects her will be that he opens the door of his pickup truck for her and helps her in. Zach arrives excited, his pickup all shiny and polished. Unfortunately, Zach's mom hasn't told him anything about the importance of opening the door for Mary. When they get to the truck, Mary stands expectantly by the passenger side door. Zach runs around to the driver's side, jumps in, guns the engine, and says, "Let's go! We'll be late for the movie!" What will Mary do? I suspect she will go ahead and climb into the pickup, deciding not to worry about her mom's comment.

They have a great time at the movie, but when Mary gets home, her mom asks whether Zach opened the door for her or not. Mary says no, that Zach forgot, but that she is sure that he will remember the next time they go out. Unfortunately, since Mary has said nothing to Zach about the importance of opening her door, the next time they go out, the same thing happens.

At this point, Mary begins to feel anxious, caught between her mother's expectations and Zach's behavior. If she doesn't say anything to Zach, she is either going to have to lie to her mother, which she doesn't like to do, or confront the fact that she is settling for less than her mother thinks she should. What could Mary do to change the situation?

One option is dumping the blame on her mother by telling Zach, "Mom says you're supposed to open the door for me." She could also use a Push technique by saying, "Please open the door for me," or "You are supposed to open the door for me." She might use a Share Path message by saying "I'm feeling uncomfortable, because I thought you would open the door for me as a sign of respect and courtesy."

Any of these might work, but for the sake of the story, let's say that Zach responds to Mary's comment with an attitude. Zach says, "Mary, your mom is a very nice lady, but she's pretty old-fashioned. Back in the old days, it was considered polite for men to open the door for women and treat them as if they were in some way superior. However, it was all for show. Men wouldn't even let women vote or work outside the home in those days. In modern times, we operate as equals. We both have good strong arms and we both can open our own doors. I don't like doing stuff I think is silly just because your mom thinks I should."

Now Mary is really feeling caught between her mom and Zach. If she sides with Zach, she realizes her mother is never going to be very happy with him. So, she decides Zach needs to open the door for the sake of future peace in the family. Mary says assertively, "Zach, you're right. I had wanted you to open the door just because my mom told me it was important. But now, after thinking about it, I realize that it is important to me too. I would like you to open the door for me, please!"

Zach is frustrated. Opening the door is against his principles, but they are late to the movie and Mary doesn't seem to be budging. She is still standing firmly outside the door of the pickup. Finally, Zach turns off the engine, stomps around to her side of the truck, yanks the door open, and says, "Hop in, Your Highness. Anything you want!" He slams the door behind her after she gets in.

Now what should Mary do? Zach accommodated her expectations, but he also treated her disrespectfully in another way. This double message puts Mary in a bind. If she meekly says thank you, Zach learns he can vent his emotions on her as long as he does what she asks. If she cuts her date short and goes home, she has lost her date and perhaps the relationship.

Let's see what happens if Mary uses her *Love Work* skills to deal with both parts of the double message:

Mary relaxes, takes a deep breath and says, "Zach, I can tell from the way you came around your truck and from what you said to me that I made you mad when I asked you to do something for me that you think is silly. Yet you did what I asked anyway. You must like me an awful lot to do that. Thank you!" She leans over and gives him a little kiss on the cheek.

What is going to happen on next week's date? There is a good chance Zach will open the door for Mary without argument. Somehow Mary managed to get around the double message, accommodate her mother's expectations, and get her own desires met. How did she do all that? First, she used her Search Path to reduce the emotional pressure Zach was carrying as a result of the Push she gave to have Zach open the door. Then she Rewarded his opening the door for her by recognizing that he had accommodated her request, even though it was difficult for him.

The issue still remains that Zack treated her with anger and sarcasm when Mary stood up for herself. Emotional pressure between them abruptly increased with her Push to get Zach to open the door. While Mary recognized Zack's feelings, which helped reduce the pressure Zach carries, Zack has yet to recognize hers. Mary is still likely to be carrying an emotional load.

To reduce this emotional pressure, Mary can use her Share Path to productively change the focus to her feelings and how Zach's behavior impacts them. She could begin a conversation about Zach's behavior by saying, "I'm feeling uncomfortable because you were mean to me when I stood up for myself. I'm anxious that you may act this way again the next time we disagree." This will challenge Zach to see how his behavior affects her, and lead to a conversation about her expectations for her treatment and care beyond opening car doors.

While it is a good idea to find out early how a potential partner is going to handle a disagreement, there are other ways Mary could have handled the door situation without escalating to a confrontation. What would have happened if Mary had begun with a Share Path message focused on her feelings, rather than using her assertive Push to get Zach to open the door? To do this, she might have said, "Zach, I'm feeling anxious and caught between your expectations and my Mom's. I realize that you don't think opening the door is important, but I want my Mom to like you, and she's not going to if you won't extend to me what she sees as common courtesy. So it is important to me as well that you open the door for me." Since Zach likes Mary and is concerned about reducing her anxiety, he's likely to open the door to meet her needs.

While we have focused on the negotiations between Zach and Mary as they begin to establish their relationship, *Love Work* skills also might be useful between Mary and her mother. Mary might well be feeling uncomfortable emotional pressure when she faces her mother's intrusive questions concerning her night out with Zach. How might her relationship with Zach have changed if she had begun a Share Path conversation with her mother by saying, "Mom, I think you have strong feelings about how Zach should behave because you want to protect me"? After a conversation around that guess, Mary could have followed with a Share Path statement such as, "I get uncomfortable when you try to manage my relationship with my date because I would like to work out the rules for my relationship with Zach myself." Mary might then have gained sufficient freedom from her mother to be more flexible and relaxed in how she deals with Zach.

Love Work Strategy Summary: When to Use Each Skill

Here is a summary of how you can use *Love Work* skills together. When your partner is upset and needs calming, use your Search Path until your partner feels calm and understood. If your partner seems stuck in negative emotions, you can help change your partner's focus by looking for an emotional Turning Point. This is when you explore what your partner is yearning for instead. In this way you can open new possibilities that move beyond what your partner is upset about.

When you personally are upset and need calming, you can use your Share Path to get your partner's attention. If your partner is too caught up in their own concerns to give you attention, return to your Search Path to calm your partner further and make sure you understand what is stressing them. Then try your Share Path again.

When both of you feel calm and understood, but the problem remains, be willing to be assertive. State what you need from your partner, and why you need it. Because this is a Push technique, you will be wise to minimize your partner's resistance to your push by remembering to acknowledge and respect your partner's needs and feelings as well. If your partner accommodates you, Reward them. Thank them for their accommodation. If they resist, return to your Search Path and explore further. Then brainstorm with your partner to find alternative options together that might meet both of your needs. If you can find no meeting point, consider taking turns, flipping a coin, postponing the decision, or exploring resources for other possible options. Be patient, rather than moving quickly to an I-win-you-lose solution, which leaves you cut off from each other. If you must make a unilateral decision, be prepared to return later to your Search Path with your partner in order to deal with the emotional pressure that your decision has created.

Using All Your *Love Work* Skills

You change old negative habits when you establish new ones in their place. Practicing these three skill sets will make your relationships much more comfortable.

A) Use your **Search Path** to reduce emotional pressure between you and your partner. Remember to guess you partner's feelings and reasons for them. Then adjust your guess based on your partner's response. Continue this process until your partner relaxes and believes you understand them.

B) Use your **Share Path** to make your partner aware of your own needs. Remember to let your partner know your feelings and why you have them. Depending on your partner's reaction to your statement, clarify your **Share Path** further. If you get resistance, move back to your **Search Path**. When you are both feeling calm and connected, move on to your **Action Path**.

C) Use an **Action Path** to influence your partner's behavior in each situation. Try each of the 6 ways to change behavior that you have learned: Bribe, Push, Punish, Reward, Push/ Reward, and Model.

Below are 7 conflict situations in which you might find yourself. Use your skills to resolve each situation in conversations with your partner or an interested friend. Keep notes on what you tried and what worked best.

Love Work game for Chapter 9:
Practice Using All Your Skills

1) Your partner can't decide what to wear to a friend's wedding. It's getting late…

Search Path____________________________________

____

Share Path _____________________________________

____

Action Path ____________________________________

____

____

2) Your spouse came home from work unusually silent, then yelled at the kids for something trivial. Little Jackson is crying…

Search Path____________________________________

____

Share Path _____________________________________

____

Action Path ____________________________________

____

____

3) You're feeling stressed about preparation for your presentation tomorrow. Your partner seems to be feeling romantic…

Search Path_______________________________

____

Share Path _______________________________

____

Action Path ______________________________

____

____

4) Your spouse has given you a fantastic meal. Usually you do the dishes, but you are feeling totally exhausted…

Search Path_______________________________

____

Share Path _______________________________

____

Action Path ______________________________

____

____

5) You would like some of your partner's attention. They want to play video games…

Search Path________________________________

____

Share Path ________________________________

____

Action Path ________________________________

____

____

6) You are trying to fix supper. The kids are fighting. Your partner just turns the TV up louder…

Search Path________________________________

____

Share Path ________________________________

____

Action Path ________________________________

____

____

Increase Your Self Awareness

What happened to your level of tension as you tried each strategy to get your needs met?

Which strategies led to better resolutions of the problem? Why?

Which **Action Path** strategy do you habitually try when first confronted with an unexpected conflict situation?

How can you reduce the emotional pressure you may have created when you used your **Action Path** choice?

Using *Love Work* for Real

Love Work skills can be a big help in reducing emotional pressure, allowing you to reconnect, and act in harmony as a couple. But to keep the skills, you have to use them. You may feel anxious at first when you tackle real relationships and real emotions. It is okay to approach real life situations slowly. Some people find it helpful to begin by giving their partner a signal that they are feeling the need to reduce emotional pressure and reconnect. Remember the story in Chapter 2 about Old Jake and the people in heaven and hell with no elbows? One couple I know simply point to their own elbows to initiate a *Love Work* conversation.

It helps to first reduce anxiety by recognizing what is going well in your relationship and the efforts your partner has been making to contribute to it.

Then, try going back and re-examining old disagreements you have had in the past. Notice when each of you fell into Protect Mode. Then talk about ways you could have used your Search Path to move yourselves to Connect Mode.

Next, try using your Search Path to talk through difficult situations in which you have found yourselves recently. Initially, use issues in which you don't have a big personal stake, so that you will find it easier to stay out of Protect Mode while you are learning to use the skill.

Finally, when you are feeling brave, try using your Search Path with current conflicts. When you think issues between you have been resolved, be sure and check in with your partner and see how your efforts have left them feeling. Their reactions will be the best indicator of your skill mastery and whether you still have some work to do. Then reward yourselves for a job well done!

Focus Questions for Chapter 9

1) When you and your partner disagree, why is it a good idea, when possible, to use your Search Path and Share Path first, before using your Action Path?

2) What is a double message? How can you use *Love Work* skills to clarify the confusion double messages create?

3) When you **Push** your partner to do something and they accommodate you, how can you keep their new behavior going without having to continue pushing?

4) When you both understand each other but continue to disagree, what are ways to deal with your conflict?

What's Next?

Chapter 10 will offer you resources for dealing with snags you may run into as you begin to use your *Love Work* skills regularly in everyday life.

Notes to Myself

Notes to Myself

Notes to Myself

164

Chapter 10
Troubleshooting:
Frequently Asked Questions

Love Work provides valuable skills for creating and maintaining stable productive relationships. However, life is a big, complicated place and couples are still likely to run into issues that they see no way to resolve. Chapter 10 offers couples help in dealing with many common questions from a *Love Work* perspective

How do we find our special partner in the first place?

Sometimes falling in love is fast and dramatic. Through some miracle, we recognize our true soulmate. Someone triggers in us a balm for our loneliness, a sense that we have always known each other, that this other person is home, a completion of the parts of us that have been missing. However, sometimes our prospective partner may be less sure. What feels right to one of us may not feel right to the other. Then our hopes are dashed, and we find ourselves dealing with broken hearts and need for further searching.

Even when both partners have that same wonderful exhilarating experience, it still contains some illusion. When we are lonely, if a few pieces fit, it is easy to make assumptions that the rest of the pieces will fit as well. As time goes by, we probably will find out that a number of pieces don't fit very well after all. We come from two different families with different values and different ways of managing our lives. So learning to fit together comfortably takes time and a lot of mutual adjustment.

Then, there is the "buyer's remorse" problem. When we buy the first car on the lot, later we are likely to see others that we think might have suited us better. The same goes with relationships. As the old saying goes, "Grass is always greener on the other side of the fence." After making our choice, it is easy to notice other people we think might have been a better fit than the person we chose. So, sticking with the commitment we have made takes self-discipline.

Making a commitment also makes us a target. True loves are in short supply. When someone meets those needs within us that have long needed fulfillment, we get a wonderful oxytocin and serotonin boost. These brain chemicals make us feel great and it shows! Suddenly, everyone finds us attractive. So here we are, attempting to create a boundary containing this one other person and no other, and suddenly other voices are inviting us to take down that fence and build one with them instead. Our professed commitment to each other only becomes a reality as we withstand temptations to break it.

Finally, exploring a new relationship is rarely a steady, one-direction process. We learn how to connect with others more the way a toddler explores a new environment. The child clings to mom, a familiar source of comfort, to gather strength. He then toddles off to see what's out there in the world across the room. A few minutes later, the child gets a little anxious, and runs back to mom. Then, having gotten reassurance, the child goes off to explore again, a little further this time.

The same thing happens when we face a new relationship. We have reached maturity and developed a sense of ourselves as individuals. Now, here's someone inviting us to share our lives with them. We may explore and like what we find, but we don't know what the unspoken expectations and responsibilities are in this new relationship. We face growing anxiety that we will get swallowed and lose our newly realized independence. Then, our need for self-protection kicks in, and we begin desiring some space. The child within starts running back to the security of being one's own person without the complications of another. We get distant, and our new partner's feelings get hurt. When our partner fears losing us and tries to hold us more closely than we desire, they can turn our natural need for some distance at times into fear that we are trapped. This may cause us to want to escape the relationship entirely.

These dynamics can happen in either direction. If it is our partner who is seeking distance, we may seek to hang onto them instead and find ourselves feeling abandoned as they try to escape our clutches. In either case, we find ourselves back playing alone in the safety of our own smaller world again, where we don't have to share. But now we are lonely once more, and our jilted partner is hurt and mad at us, or vice versa.
We can escape these struggles by using our *Love Work* skills to temper uncomfortable feelings of fear of too much closeness on one hand, and fear of isolation and loneliness on the other. Over time, we learn to match the ebb and flow of our partner's needs with our own, just as they learn to accommodate ours. We gain confidence that pulling away does not mean that our partner is escaping. They just need more space for a while. We grow closer to each other most easily when we allow those we love to feel safe and welcome at their own pace, rather than attempt to force their closeness.

Developing a healthy, stable relationship is a lot like cooking "slow food." The best meal takes time to prepare. Relationship rush jobs may stave off loneliness for the time being, but often self-destruct–or, if they survive, do so only after a long period of insecurity.

Confidence in our commitment is built by our relationship's survival over time. It is through surviving the rough spots together that we gain confidence that our partner is really there for us.

Staying on Track:
"We get busy with other things and fall back into old destructive patterns. How do we keep on track?"

Often couples use *Love Work* skills until they feel comfortable with each other. Then they move on to other, more pressing concerns while their *Love Work* skills slowly atrophy. After a time, when emotional pressure builds again, the couple may find that they have forgotten how to get back on track. This is treating relationships like a bad back: We only remember to do our exercises when we feel pain. Back problems respond much better when we stick to a regular exercise program even when we are feeling fine.

In the same way, relationships fare much better when we set aside time to check in with each other a regular basis. It might be once a day, once a week, or once a month as our needs require. To make sure it happens, some people write the date and time in their calendars and include a reward they both enjoy afterwards. Regular use of Search Path skills keeps our relationships fresh and alive. Once budding problems have been dealt with, we can make it a time to dream together and make plans for our future. In this way, our lives together will become more intentional and less reactive.

Learning Patience:
What should we do when our efforts to understand each other's feelings don't seem to be getting anywhere?

Feelings don't always cooperate on our time schedule. Sometimes we may find that seeking to understand our partner's feelings doesn't seem to be working. Perhaps the feelings being expressed are a mixed-up hodgepodge that does't make sense, or our partner just shuts down. We may find we are both getting more upset and frustrated rather than reaching mutual understanding and resolution.

Often this happens because we are pushing for feelings rather than relaxing and letting feelings reveal themselves in their own time. We may need to take a break and let things ripen for a while. We may not understand what is going on inside or between us until we have digested what we have discussed and have given our feelings time to settle.

Feelings are a lot like squirrels in a park. A child might want to catch a squirrel and try hard by chasing every squirrel they can find. How many do they catch? None! Squirrels get nervous when they notice someone after them, and they keep their distance.

On the other hand, if we stopped chasing squirrels for a minute, we might notice the old man sitting on a park bench and not chasing squirrels at all. But there is a squirrel sitting on his knee and another is rooting in his pockets. How does he do that? The old man is sitting calm and quiet, letting the squirrels come to him... and he has peanuts! When a squirrel happens to come close, he flicks a peanut its way. The squirrels soon relax and regard him as a source of nourishment rather than a potential threat.

Because humans are social creatures, the peanut we have to offer is our attention. Because feelings are like wild things that tend to run and hide when we chase them, we are more likely to find them when we don't rush after them but quietly give feelings our patient attention until the feelings relax and begin to reveal themselves in their own time.

Deciding Who Fixes Things: "Whose responsibility is it to deal with emotions in our relationship?"

Frequently, when a couple is in conflict, both members carry uncomfortable emotional loads. Yet neither partner is willing to take the first step to reduce pressure, because each sees the problem as the other person's fault. In theory, the calmest person is most able to start the process of pressure reduction, because that person is more able to calm their own Protect Mode reaction and instead imagine what their partner's point of view might be.

However, if our partner doesn't happen to do this, it is best that we be willing to take the first step. Why? Because someone needs to begin the process, and we alone have control over our own behavior. If we wait for our partner to seek peace first, we give our partner control of our relationship at a time when our partner may be upset with us. If our partner is caught up in Protect Mode, they are unlikely to be thinking about our best interests. We take care of ourselves as well as our partner when we use the skills we have been learning to calm the stress between us.

We begin by using our Search Path. Once our partner has calmed down and feels understood, we can move to our Share Path skills. This way we can present our own point of view in a way that doesn't leave our partner feeling under attack.

Using the same reasoning, let's review whose responsibility it is:

- To calm ourselves into Connect Mode? Ours.

- To get our partner out of Protect Mode? Ours.

- To set limits on what we can handle? Ours.

- To state what we need from your partner? Ours.

The more we take responsibility for our life and our relationships, the more likely they are to go in directions we desire.

Choosing the Right Time and Place: "What do I do if my partner is hyper-focused on the problem and gets impatient when I try to use my Search Path?"

The Search Path is counterintuitive in that it helps couples deal with problems by focusing on the couple's process of interaction, rather than focusing on the problem itself. Since couples in distress are often hyper-focused on problems they cannot resolve, they can easily get frustrated and leave relationship-building efforts prematurely if those problems aren't addressed first. Unfortunately, the couple's hyper-focus on the problem is likely to be part of the problem. Couples solve problems best when they feel calm and connected.

So your partner may get frustrated when you try to focus on feelings at a time when they think dealing with the problem at hand is what is important. Your partner might respond impatiently, "Yeah, that's how I'm feeling! Now what are you going to do about it?" Then you, the Listener, will be tempted to leap into an attempt to "do something about it." But at this point you are likely to feel off-balance and defensive. Instead, you could take a slow breath, self-calm, and once again use your Search Path to guess how your partner must be feeling to make such a demand. Your response might be, "It looks like you are anxious about this and you think I might have a quick solution…"

The first step in solving a problem as a team is becoming a team in the first place. Your Search Path is a process for achieving that connection. If your partner's idea of the quick fix is something you are uncomfortable with, you can use your Share Path to express your reservations without getting into a pushing contest. When you and your partner are feeling calm and connected, solutions to difficult problems more often become possible.

Use your judgment in deciding when to use your *Love Work* skills. Sometimes you may have to put feelings aside temporarily because time is short, there is an emergency, or you or your partner lack the emotional resources to invest in relationship building at that time. However, you will need to come back to feelings eventually. Emotional pressure is likely to remain a disruptive influence in your relationship until you take time to reduce it.

Dealing with Blame:
"What should I do when my partner puts me on the spot with questions that are impossible to answer?"

You are likely to move into Protect Mode when your partner refuses to accept your answers to their "impossible to answer" questions: "How can I ever trust you again?," for example. Rather than attempting to answer a question that you cannot answer successfully, you can avoid the trap if you use your Search Path to calm the emotional pressure behind the question. In this way, you can help your partner relax and come to grips with what is bothering them.

To do this, first take a breath and relax yourself. Then think about how your partner might be feeling to prompt the question. Your Search Path guess might be something like this: "It sounds like you are feeling terribly discouraged and distrustful because I've let you down in the past. You don't see a way that I can regain your trust. That must be a hard load for you to bear."

Await a response. After your partner replies, encourage further pressure reduction by saying, "Tell me more."

Once you have attended your partner's negative feelings for a while, you can try a Turning Point guess about what your partner is yearning for instead. For example, suppose your partner has been complaining that you have let them down. The Turning Point in your Search Path might be, "It sounds like you are longing for the level of trust we used to share, because it made you feel happy…" This shifts the focus from negative feelings to a positive goal. This change in the conversation begins building hope and direction for your future together.

Often the unanswerable question is actually a request for reassurance. That may be something you cannot give with a direct answer. In the example we are using, the painful truth is that if you have violated your partner's trust, you cannot just say you are sorry and be done with it, no matter how good your intentions are. After all, since you have violated trust in the past, neither you nor your partner knows whether you can be trustworthy in the future. Only your success at being trustworthy over time will rebuild trust for both of you. Until then, following your Search Path helps you carry that load of uncertainty together as a team.

Getting Your Partner's Attention: "What do I do when I want my partner to listen to me, but they are not interested?"

If you have been trying to get your partner's attention to no avail, try using your Search Path to find out what is going on with your partner. This may be difficult for you because it means postponing getting your own needs met still longer. However, your Search Path will help you find out what is going on with your partner that prevents them from taking care of you. In the process, you also create a calm, receptive environment in which you partner is more likely to listen to you in return. You may discover your partner doesn't have the time or the emotional resources to take care of you at that moment. If not, decide on a time to talk that might be better. If you discover your partner is feeling fine but isn't aware that you are carrying a load, try using your Share Path by telling your partner how you are feeling and the reason you have those feelings. This way, you may gain your partner's cooperation without making them feel pushed around. To use this skill effectively, review Share Path communication described in Chapter 6.

Getting Your Partner's Cooperation: "What if my partner won't do what I want them to?"

This "Will/Won't Problem" frequently occurs in couple relationships. A familiar adage for encouraging self-discipline is "Where there is a *will*, there is a *way*!" However, in relationships this philosophy often causes more problems than it solves. A couple is made up of two different people with two different sets of goals and two different approaches for getting things done. As soon as we try to push our purposes onto our partner, we are asking our partner to sacrifice their own perspective (which they can clearly see) for ours (of which they may be only dimly aware). Hence, unless our goals happen to align, we are likely to meet resistance.

Thus, a more accurate statement for couples trying to get each other to do things is, "Where there is a *will*, there is a *won't*!" So, we are likely to meet with resistance when we try to get our partner to do something that we desire, but in which they have no special interest. The "will" is what we desire. The "won't" is what we are asking our partner to give up in order to accommodate our need. The greater our partner's interest in their own personal goal, the greater will be their resistance to setting it aside in order to take care of our agenda.

So, when you meet with resistance, before pushing your partner harder, first try putting your own concerns on hold temporarily. Instead, use your Search Path to reduce any emotional pressure that your partner might be carrying and to discover their conflicting goals. Doing this paves the way for your partner to be willing to listen to your concerns in return. Then, use your Share Path to convey to your partner what you need from them. Now your partner will be more likely to invest in a solution to help reduce the emotional load you carry as well, since you have first done that favor for them.

Keeping Your Cool:
"What should I do if I try to follow my Search Path, but I get upset?"

Assuming that your partner is also angry, once you get upset you are unlikely to make much progress solving the problem until you both calm down. So, it is time to take a break… but be sure to plan time to come back and try again, so your partner doesn't feel abandoned. Then go burn off some adrenaline. Run, split wood, lift weights, do sit-ups. Think large muscle exercise. Adrenaline is meant for use. It primes your muscles for fight or flight. But it is bad for your health and your relationships to carry it locked up inside. If your partner won't let the problem drop, then go for a run anyway. Your partner will have to run as well in order to keep arguing. If your partner does choose to run with you, don't worry. It is hard to argue while you are running.

During the time that you take a break from your disagreement, take some time to think about the issues calmly. Then find a piece of paper. Draw a heart at the top and write "I Care for You" inside it. Below the heart begin your Search Path by writing down how you each think your partner is feeling and your understanding of the reason your partner might have those feelings. Then write down your Share Path in which you name your own feelings about the topic and reasons for them. Begin your next conversation on the problem topic by telling your partner what you wrote. Continue your Search Paths with each other to explore your different points of view. Return to using the paper with the heart on it as the need arises to help you keep a caring focus on your partner. Once you both feel heard and understood, it becomes much easier to look for solutions as a team that satisfy both of your needs.

Finding Our Peaceful Center:
"How can we find our calm space, so we can use our Search Path more effectively?"

It is there. We all have the gift: that quiet voice within, behind the thunder and tumult. But we have to wait for it. It is not a demanding voice, but it remains a steady presence when we take time to listen for it and act in harmony with it. Prayer can help. We simply ask the Spiritual Power greater than ourselves, however we define it, for the gift of peace, then wait for it to come. Many other calming disciplines are helpful as well. Meditation is an effective way to become more aware of the calm present moment surrounding us, within and without, rather than focusing so intently on the alarm calls of problems. Yoga is good for us physically and spiritually. It encourages mindfulness, muscle tone, and flexibility, plus it builds the emotional discipline to endure a certain amount of discomfort.

When we actively seek quiet spaces in our lives, it encourages their growth within us. When we become aware of people, places, and activities that increase our sense of peace, and take time to seek them out, our inner lives begin to reflect that peace as well.

Peace comes when we feel in control of our internal state. We do this best when we reduce our reliance on external sources for our emotional comfort such as nonstop entertainment, constant cell phone use, and compulsive social stimulation. This also includes reducing dependence on drugs and alcohol, including stimulants such as caffeine and nicotine, and relaxants such as sleeping pills and pain killers.

Self-calming is a discipline, like learning to play an instrument. It takes practice. It also takes courage. We aren't used to quiet. We may fear the thoughts and feelings that await us when we stop our rush through existence. We can enjoy eternity now, in the present moment. When we rush, we miss much.

Lengthening a Short Fuse:
"What if we get defensive so quickly that we automatically begin to fight?"

To listen effectively to our partner, we need the skill of putting our own perspective on hold while we calmly attend our partner. If we are highly reactive and unable to restrain ourselves, we will not be able to listen to our partner long enough for our partner to feel heard and understood. If our partner reacts similarly towards us, our attempts at communication can easily turn into a fight. Fortunately, there are many things we can do to develop our ability to calm our emotions, so we can pay better attention to our partner.

First, we can practice our Search Path exercises until we are so comfortable with the process that we can use it even when we feel under pressure. Like learning to play an instrument, using our Search Path becomes easy with practice. We would feel pretty uncomfortable if we were called on to perform with our local band if we hadn't practiced the music. In the same way, if we simply understand how the Search Path works, but we haven't practiced it, we are likely to be uncomfortable using it when we really need the skill. In which case, we are likely to abandon our Search Path just when we really need it and fall back on former, more comfortable but also more destructive behavior patterns. When we have practiced our Search Path enough to use it easily, simply having confidence that we can use the skill helps us stay calm.

We are likely to have difficulty staying calm if we or our partner are extremely stressed and at the end of our emotional resources. In such a situation, we will have difficulty focusing on anything but our own survival. We may be exhausted and dealing with difficult external environmental issues such as being overwhelmed by work, experiencing financial difficulties, or facing some other ongoing stressful situation.

We may be dealing with internal environmental difficulties. These might include substance abuse, health issues, or adrenaline overload caused by video games, playing the stock market compulsively, or other stresses. So, it is worth taking a frank assessment of our lifestyles and practice taking good care of ourselves.

Some people turn to substances such as caffeine, nicotine, alcohol, marijuana, sedatives, and other mood-altering drugs in order to get calmed down and find relief from stress. However, when it comes to managing relationship issues, these are rarely effective solutions. There is this time lag problem. When difficulties arise, we need ways to calm ourselves at that moment, not some time later when our drug of choice finally kicks in. These drugs also have the unfortunate side effect of altering brain function. We manage Connect Mode best when our brains are in a steady state, rather than getting jerked around with various drugs.

Psychotropic drugs our doctor may prescribe are in a different category and can be helpful. They take effect very slowly, and we take them regularly over a long period of time so that our brains can achieve a new steady state.

While we may expect our partner to assume some responsibility for our care, we will be the one who experiences the consequences of our physical, emotional, and spiritual deterioration if we haven't been taking care of ourselves. So we each need to assume primary responsibility for our own health and happiness. This includes our being willing to ask for help from our partner when we need it. When both we and our partner are involved in our care, but we ourselves are in charge, we are more likely to feel calm and secure.

There are other things we can do to lower our emotional volatility. When we sense any sort of attack on our security, even something as simple as an unfeeling remark from our partner, we are likely to move into Protect Mode, with its resultant adrenaline overload. We need ways to use up the adrenaline buildup that we develop in emotionally tense situations. Our bodies make adrenaline to activate our muscles in case we need to fight or escape an enemy threat. However, threats we perceive in our modern world, like a letter from the IRS in the mail, often require brain work, not muscle work. So we need ways to get rid of excess adrenaline other than getting out our spear and battle axe. Large muscle exercise such as walking, running, swimming, working out, and playing sports, rather than just watching them, do the job. Exercise is not just good for your body. It is good for your relationships as well. As your muscles tire and your adrenaline level lowers, you are more likely to relax and be ready to connect with your partner.

Some people have demanding physical jobs that work them hard and leave them exhausted, yet they are still stressed rather than relaxed when they arrive home. This is because the job is pushing them, causing additional adrenaline overload. Our calming exercise needs to be deliberate, not just reactive. We relax best when we go for a run because we choose to, not because we have to. Our exercise benefits us more and our lives feel more under our control when *we have things to do* rather than when *we have to do things*. So our exercise should move us into a world of choice, rather than merely be a response to the demands of our situation.

We can choose a relaxing place to get our exercise. A jog in the park will have greater benefit than jogging on a tread mill. Bicycling in heavy traffic or watching a violent movie while pumping an exercise machine won't do as much to reduce our adrenaline load or lower our reactivity as will a hike along a scenic path.

We are most stable and least reactive emotionally when our security is diversified. When we have lots of secure connections in our lives, we will be less likely to find ourselves overwhelmed and out of control when our relationship with our partner gets stressed. As a result, we will be more able to stay out of our Protect Mode and more able to pull our partner out of theirs. Thus it is worth investing in connections within our community such as book clubs, churches, and community support groups. Other options include building strong relations with family and friends, increasing expertise in our vocation, getting enough sleep, eating a healthy diet, contributing to our society, planning for our future, helping little old ladies across the street, or anything else that connects us to our friends, community, and our sense of meaning and purpose.

We don't need to do all these things at once. But when an opportunity comes, it is worth investing in it. Once begun, new healthy life habits tend to take on lives of their own with only small additional effort on our part.

Sometimes, because of difficult past circumstances, some people develop highly reactive thought patterns that get in the way of their attempts to calm themselves. Meditation, yoga, and other mindfulness disciplines can help with this. There are also self-help books that can help. For example, Laurel Mellin's book *Wired For Joy* offers a guide for individual emotional brain training that can help change and calm our automatic responses.

Because many of our mental habits were formed in relationship with our parents or other important people in our lives, a personal touch can also help us change them. Help from a calm mentor, pastor, professional counselor, or psychotherapist can help us change ingrained mental patterns that cause us difficulties.

Fortunately, even when we do go into Protect Mode, there are always paths back to our calm Connect Mode. When we or our partner recognize that we have gotten triggered and can no longer talk constructively, it helps to take time out to calm back down and think about the issue, while setting a time to revisit the topic. At that time, we can resume following our Search Paths with each other until we both feel fully heard and understood.

This can help us slow down our argument and turn it into a caring conversation.

Breaking Through a Stone Wall: "How do I make my partner listen to reason?"

The problem is probably occurring because you are attempting to reason with a partner who is in Protect Mode. When a person is in Protect Mode, their "lizard brain" will be in charge. So your partner's thinking will be operating at a reactive emotional level rather than at an intellectual level. In such a situation, your rational explanation will be as useless as trying to explain to a frightened pet why it is OK to get a rabies shot. Your pet's emotional brain doesn't reason. Neither does your emotional brain or your partner's.

As you get frustrated because your partner is not responding to your efforts at being reasonable, you are likely to move into your own Protect Mode as well. Then communication will break down entirely. The way out of this difficulty is to first take a break to calm down. When you return to the conversation, begin by using your Search Path to calm and connect with your partner. Once you are both operating in Connect Mode and understand each other's point of view, the conversation is more likely to become reasonable and, better yet, effective.

Getting Close and Personal:
How can we apply *Love Work* skills in the bedroom?

Sex is a lovely way to relax with each other and increase our emotional connection. However, when our relationship is under stress, sex can also be a time when anxiety and hurt feelings can surface, leaving us feeling isolated and alone in spite of close physical contact.

The same *Love Work* skills apply with sex as they do in other aspects of our lives. When issues causing emotional pressure in our relationships have not been dealt with, they may intrude in the bedroom like an unwelcome visitor at this most inopportune time. What an awkward decision to face! If we ignore these issues, sex can become a distant mechanical act, leaving neither partner satisfied. But if we bring the issues up, we may ruin the mood.

The best approach is, of course, to deal with these issues long before love making, so that emotional pressure is already low when we desire physical connection. Otherwise, Protect Mode thoughts can create emotional distance even though our bodies are physically close. *Love Work* skills can help us lower the pressure, so we can relax and enjoy each other. If we have put off dealing with uncomfortable issues until we are in bed, bringing them up at that point is likely be a rude awakening for our partner. One way to deal with this is to let our partner know there are things we need to talk about but set a time for talking later. However, our partner may say, "No! If there are issues standing between us, let's talk now." If that is the case, take time for the detour. Low emotional pressure definitely fills love making with greater pleasure.

As hormones rise during love making, thoughts and fantasies may appear that we may fear are unacceptable to our partner. Often it is worth the risk to share what is going on with our partner. We may open unexpected new dimensions in our love life. If not, using our Search Path can get back us on track and deepen our mutual understanding.

Performance anxiety is another issue that can interfere with a lovely time in bed. We may be distracted by fears that we won't satisfy our partner or that we won't be satisfied. If we have a wonderful time, we may worry that unrealistic expectations are being set for the future. Again, Love Work skills can get those worries out where they can be understood and calmed.

Education can help deal with unrealistic expectations in our sex life. No, we don't have to have climaxes at the same time, or even have a climax at all for love making to be full of pleasure. Women typically need more time to be aroused. Men need to learn patience. Getting a book on the subject and reading up can make us a lot more fun to be with.

We can use *Love Work* skills to negotiate a time, place, and pace for love making. We can use them to make our desires known in a way that invites mutual cooperation. For example, here is a Share Path invitation: "I'm missing your soft touch… Maybe we could set aside some special time for each other…?"

Love Work skills can help as we become comfortable enough with each other to move beyond words and enter the world of sensation. Our bodies are loaded with touch receptors. Some areas have very few and don't get much response. Other areas of our body are so loaded that we must be very relaxed and trusting to have them explored at all. Here are *Love Work* strategies we can use to discover what is pleasurable for our partner, and what is a turn off:

" I'm guessing you like being touched here, like this…" (Search Path)

" Not so fast… Slow way down, Love. I need to be relaxed to really enjoy you. How about a nice neck and shoulder rub to begin with…" (Share Path)

"Hon, that's a little too hard…! Aah, that's just right…" (Share Path)

"I imagine you like to be touched like this… Maybe here, to start with… No… ticklish, huh? How about here instead, and I rub a little more gently… slowly…" (Search Path).

We are built to enjoy each other. In Connect Mode, we can celebrate this special part of our lives!

Dealing with a Control Freak:
"What if my partner pressures me to do things I don't wish to do?"

Here, you are on the receiving end of the Will/Won't Problem. You feel resistant to your partner's push, but you probably feel anxious or guilty as well, because you like to make your partner happy. If you push back, you worry that things will escalate into a fight. If you let your partner have their way, you encourage more pushing. Then you will feel bad for not standing up for yourself, and your partner will learn to discount your feelings as unimportant.

The way out of this fight/flight trap is, once again, to follow your Search Path. Calm yourself with a slow breath. Then, imagine how your partner must be feeling to push you about the matter at hand, and the reason they might be feeling that way. Tell your partner your guess and wait. This takes your partner's focus off of pushing you around and encourages them to look at how they are feeling instead. This is a more comfortable position for you and a more productive one for your partner.

You may also be able set limits with a Share Path approach. Using this approach, you might say, "I'm uncomfortable with what you are asking me to do because I haven't had a chance to think about it. Why don't I sleep on it, and we can talk about it more tomorrow after dinner?" Either approach will give you some room to regain your balance and perspective. Having time to think may also give you a chance to develop solutions that meet both of your needs.

Risking Openness:
"What if I have secrets that I can't share for fear of losing my partner?"

Secrets are tough loads to carry for a variety of reasons. It takes energy to keep them, so you don't have that energy available for other things. Secrets make you defensive, so you tend to stay in Protect Mode and feel on edge. Secrets cause emotional distance in your relationship and block spontaneity and intimacy with your partner. They also block you from getting nurture and support from your partner. Even if your partner tries to give you love, you can't receive it because you know the person they are attempting to love isn't who you really are.

If your secret is a fling with someone else, sex with your partner often stops being fun because of guilt feelings and interfering thoughts and memories. Secrets isolate you and leave you feeling lonely. This makes you likely to do more of what you are keeping secret in order to deal with those lonely feelings.

Telling the truth sets you free of all of that. However, letting go of a false relationship to take a chance on a real one can be risky. You will have to deal with the consequences of truth, including upsetting and possibly losing your partner. As you open up, the load you have been carrying is now placed on your partner's shoulders as well.

You can help your partner bear this load by following your Search Path as you deal with your partner's reactions to your disclosure. This helps your partner realize you understand and accept responsibility for the pain you have caused and that you share that pain. Suffering with your partner because of pain you have caused will take patience on your part. If you have dropped a bombshell, it is likely to take time for your partner to grieve the loss of the person they thought you were and come to accept the reality of the person you are. Since you made the mistake that led to the secret, your responsibility in repairing the damage includes standing firm and caring in the presence of your partner's pain and doubt as it ebbs and flows, until the wound has time to heal.

Does this mean you are required to tell the truth at all times? Use your judgment. Some things may not be central to your relationship and would best be left alone. Constant brutal honesty can be hard to live with. Sometimes you may wish to calm and reassure your partner even when you are not feeling sure yourself. You may have chosen the relationship for other reasons than emotional intimacy—financial security, for example— so a close emotional connection may not be your priority. In such a case, you may decide it is best to keep your secrets in spite of the emotional distance this creates. Sometimes there can be safety issues involved if your partner is potentially violent and your secret is your desire to leave the relationship. Such secrets are best kept until you have escaped to safety.

Finding Safety:
"What if my partner is abusive?"

How to deal with abuse from your partner depends on the level of abuse and what is causing the behavior. Abuse may stem from abusive situations you or your partner experienced growing up and revert to when under stress. It may occur when emotional tension between you and your partner reaches the breaking point. It may be the result of each of you inflicting escalating tit-for-tat punishments on the other, and neither of you being willing to negotiate or back down. If these are the types of situations causing the problem and if your conflict has reached the intensity of physical abuse, you would be wise to work on your relationship skills in the safe presence of a calm couples therapist. It is very difficult to calm Protect Mode reactions in yourself or in your partner enough to use *Love Work* skills when you have concerns about your safety.

Physical abuse also can result because a person feels unlovable, and therefore believes the only way they can keep their partner is through control, intimidation, and fear. Such people have grown up with experiences that have led them to believe that having control over the person they love is the only way they can keep themselves from being abandoned. People with addiction and dependency issues also may feel they have nothing to offer and cannot survive without their partner's help. In these cases, such people will seek to capture a partner who will protect and take care of them. Such insecure partners seek to force their partners to remain in the relationship, either consciously or unconsciously, by using a variety of strategies to make their partners feel helpless, beholden, and intimidated.

Here are two common situations in which you may find yourself if you have been caught in this type of relationship:

Your partner may attempt to isolate you from any other sources of emotional support except themselves or those sympathetic to your partner. They will be jealous and consider your having your own friends disloyal and a threat.

Your partner may try to increase your dependence on them by discouraging you from having your own job or means of support. They will promise to take care of you and the family finances. However, if your partner cannot meet your family's economic needs sufficiently, they are likely to hold you responsible and accuse you of spending too much money.

Love Work skills can help you move beyond these painful situations. But first you, the abused partner, will need to find the courage and support to escape. As long as you are their captive, your abusive partner will not be motivated to change.

Depending on your partner's level of dependency and insecurity, escape can be painful, and even dangerous. Your local Social Services Agencies usually provide information for confidential counseling and safe houses which can help you and your children safely escape abusive situations.

Once you are free and recover a sense of your own competence and independence, you can choose either to renegotiate your relationship with your partner or to move on without them. Renegotiation should include treatment for substance dependency for your partner, if that is an issue, together with couples counseling to establish new, mutually supportive relationship patterns. If your partner will not accept these conditions and you return anyway, then you are likely to fall back into the same painful patterns from which you temporarily escaped.

Affairs:
"So, I went to this conference and met somebody... I can't tell my partner what happened. Now what?"

I'm so sorry you have gotten yourself into this common, but terribly difficult situation. Affairs can happen for lots of reasons, often without any deliberate intent on anyone's part. Some examples include having too much to drink when we're by ourselves at a conference… Or having a coworker with whom we spend lots of time and find ourselves really liking… Maybe our partner is super busy all the time and we are feeling disconnected and lonely… Maybe someone looks good, we know they feel the same about us, and chemistry takes over.

It's often not a conscious decision to abandon our partner. Once hormones start raging, we may not even remember our partner is part of the equation. Maybe it's not anything that winds up in bed. The fact remains that we have developed feelings for someone who is not our partner. In our partner's eyes, we will have broken the agreement of *"I take care of you. You take care of me. We take care of each other."* We have betrayed our partner's trust. The one who committed their lives to us, who loves us and counts on our support, is going to be terribly hurt.

The services of a good marriage counselor can be a big help. When our basic security is threatened, and emotional pressure is at the breaking point, it becomes very difficult to hold our calm space well enough to find our Connect Mode. Because we have broken basic trust with our partner, we have also severely damaged our ability to help them find their Connect Mode. So, we are likely to need the calm presence of someone outside our relationship to help us calm enough to deal with the situation.

Nevertheless, it doesn't hurt to give *Love Work* skills a try. They are powerful tools. So here is a look at the decisions and difficult feelings we will face and need to deal with if we find ourselves in this predicament.

In this society, it is difficult to care well for two intimate relationships at once. We must mislead one person or the other, and living a lie is hard work. We can't really relax and have fun with our partner because we have to put energy into keeping up a false image of ourselves. We can't give our partner the affirmation they need, because the false part of ourselves doesn't really mean it. We can no longer really accept the love our partner tries to give us because we know they would not be giving us that affection if they knew who we really were. Images and thoughts of the other person will interfere in our love life with our partner. Our partner is likely to feel needy and want to know what's wrong.

So our partner wants to go to therapy. We don't! We get frustrated and scream at the kids. Our partner jumps on us for being a jerk. We get mad at them because we know we are a jerk. It can get awful very quickly. As a result, our loneliness mounts. We will be tempted to become more deeply involved with this new person because they are now the only one who really knows us as we really are.

How can we get out of this mess? If we tell our partner where things really stand, they are going to get hurt. The new person will also get hurt. There is a good chance we will get hurt, too. We may get left high and dry with neither person accepting us. If we choose one, we leave the other abandoned. We can live a lie, but then we face the loss of our intimate relationship with our partner. We will have to live with the possibility of discovery and exposure at any time. Our security is gone. Our emotional pressure is likely to remain very high until we make the choice for one partner or the other and endure the consequences of that decision.

If we choose to leave our partner, or if our partner gives up and leaves us, we will have many challenges to overcome with our new partner as well. Fling relationships rarely last. We are likely to feel guilty about breaking our commitment with our partner. But our new partner isn't going to want to hear about those feelings, since they will feel threatened by them. So, we will need to rely on our *Love Work* skills to avoid starting off our new relationship by stuffing our feelings. Also, old emotions from our old relationship don't just dissolve on command. They linger for a long time. Our new partner isn't going to want to hear about that either. So we will need to rely on our *Love Work* skills to get us beyond this too. Since we have deserted our partner, our new partner may well fear that we might desert them too. Since we no longer have confidence in our own fidelity, we are likely to have fears about our new partner's fidelity as well. As a result, both new partners are likely to feel insecure and act over-controlling. Children involved with either our old or new partner are likely to have strong feelings about what has happened. We will have continuing obligations towards them as well. All these issues increase emotional pressure and are painful burdens to bear. We can use our Search and Share Paths to reduce the emotional pressure of these burdens as we develop our new relationships. In time, it is possible to work through to calm and connection once more.

If we were married in our former relationship, there will be legal and financial tangles. *Love Work* skills can help us through these challenges, too, but things are likely to remain complicated for some time.

On the other hand, we could try to repair our relationship with our partner. The truth can set us free to build a new relationship with them, but the operation will also be painful. Everyone involved is going to hurt. Our fling partner will feel deserted. Our spouse is going to feel hurt and furious, and fearing that, in our eyes, they must be worthless since we have shown that we don't value our relationship. We can use our Share Path in humble confession to show that we understand the damage we have done and accept our responsibility for creating this mess, and for repairing it. Our Search Path can help us care for our partner's feelings through this tumult until they know we truly understand the depth of the pain we have caused. This is a hard path, but our partner will be unable to believe we still love them unless we show we are willing to stand firm and bear the pain of the emotions we have caused by our betrayal of their trust.

We will need to create a strategy to keep the problem from reccurring. Affairs can be addictive and breaking them off can be hard. When we find ourselves wanting to talk to the other person and explain things to them, we need to commit to talking to our first partner about it instead. The first time may have been a mistake. After that, it is intentional! Being willing to go see a marital/ relationship counselor is a good way to show our partner we are serious about repairing things with them. It also is a way to understand and change habits that led to the problem. Our chances for rebuilding our relationship improve greatly when we understand what went wrong the first time around, so we can avoid repeating those mistakes.

In spite of things getting better, our partner's lack of confidence in our impulse control means that they are likely to revisit the sad subject periodically. Each time, we will need to show our continued love by patiently using our Search Path until they are reassured that we still understand their pain and won't hurt them again.

As time goes on and we remain patient and true, our partner's fears will gradually relax. We will gain confidence in ourselves and pride in the success and resilience of the relationship we have created together.

Quitting:
"What if I need to give up on my relationship?"

What a terribly painful issue to face! You have invested a lot into your relationship, and you both have much to lose. Attachment loss has a painful emotional impact much like the death of a loved one. You have decided to dissolve the pact of *"I take care of you. You take care of me. We take care of each other."* But feelings don't go away just because you sign a piece of paper. Detachment comes slowly, often with much ambivalence. You may be ready to leave in the heat of the moment, then reconsider once you calm down. Once you are ready to leave, you partner's behavior may change for the better, causing you to reconsider.

Divorce should be less an escape than an organized retreat. Like a good marriage, a good divorce occurs most smoothly when both parties can cooperate. Often people considering divorce have forgotten that they still have partners and are brooding in isolation. Assuming your safety isn't threatened, you might try talking about problems you see with your partner. Here, using your Search and Share Paths can help you work out your path forward, whether toward separation or repairing your differences.

When you divorce, you no longer can turn to your partner for help dealing with the host of primal Protect Mode emotions that occur when you face being alone. These include anger, fear, loneliness, depression, resentment, and jealousy, to name a few. So, to reduce this emotional pressure, you will need to use your Share Path to develop strong connections with people you trust beyond your relationship with your partner. These might include a counselor or therapist, caring family members, friends, a religious group or a community support group.

The freedom you gain may not be all you hoped for. You will still have to deal with your own emotional baggage. You can't escape yourself. There are likely to be ways that your life will continue to involve your former partner. If you have kids, you may no longer be husband and wife, but you still remain mom and dad. You can use your Search and Share Paths to help with these issues.

When you become single again, often the friends, home, and community you shared with your partner fall away as well. Even your sense of yourself changes. You were a part of a couple. After divorce, you will have to reinvent yourself as an individual again. This takes time, and you are likely to feel unsure of yourself and awkward in your new role. It can take a number of years before you find your new normal. It will take time and effort to build new relationships and create a comfortable environment in your new situation. Using your Search and Share Paths can help you build these.

It is often helpful to discuss your situation with those you know and trust if you are thinking about taking this big step. Here, using your Share Path can help you clarify the situation. Your friends may be able to give you some perspective, suggest ways out of the dead end you are facing, as well as being sources of emotional support if you decide to go through with divorce.

Getting professional help first is well worth the cost. Individual and couples counseling can save a marriage, or help you through divorce if that is the best solution.

Make adequate preparation for the practical aspects of life after divorce before you take the plunge. How will you manage economically? Who moves? Where will you live?

Dividing stuff up gets complicated. Who gets the car? The house? Wedding treasures that were given to you both? How will you divide financial responsibilities such as debt and child support? Using Search and Share Paths with your partner can help you avoid angry expensive court battles. Mediators, or lawyers with mediation skills, can be a big help as well.

Don't decide on divorce when you are mad. Impulsive emotional decisions lose momentum as you calm down. The decision to leave your relationship is most likely to be smooth and successful when you explored other options, made it in your calm space, and prepared carefully for the change.

Involving A Higher Power: "Can my spiritual beliefs help me use *LoveWork* skills effectively?"

Love Work has not addressed spiritual beliefs and how they affect relationships. This is because people have diverse beliefs and *Love Work* aims to be broad enough in presenting the mechanics of relationships to allow a wide spectrum of people to feel comfortable using this approach. People from many different religious persuasions and those with no religious beliefs can all learn to use these tools successfully. That said, a strong spiritual life can be of great benefit in using *Love Work* since one's faith is a relationship with a force outside of your physical relationships. Because of this, you can use your stable spiritual relationship to find the calm place you need to remain in Connect Mode even when your physical relationship is threatened.

Aligning with Christian Doctrine: "Will *Love Work* support my Christian beliefs?"

You don't have to be Christian to use Love Work skills, but New Testament doctrine fits well with the *Love Work* model. For example, Paul's statements in Corinthians I, 13:12, about seeing "as through a glass, darkly, then face-to-face" and knowing "in part" and then knowing "even as we are known" have parallels in *Love Work*. When emotional tension grows in a relationship, we see each other through perceptions distorted by emotion and project onto one another our fears and preconceptions. We then fail to base our interactions with our partner on the person our partner actually is. We could call this situation "seeing through a glass darkly." This contributes to misunderstanding and pain in our relationship. When we reduce the pressure in a relationship by using our Search Path skills, we begin seeing each other "face-to-face" once again.

Paul describes love in Corinthians I, 13:7, where he says love "bears all things, believes all things, hopes all things, endures all things". This is also a good description of what *Love Work* suggests we must do to contain our own emotions while we seek to reduce the emotional pressure our partner carries.

Spiritual beliefs can also help us manage our emotional reactions and keep calm and centered rather than just reacting in Protect Mode. When we have grown up in families that exhibit out-of-control emotions, we are more likely to have difficulty controlling our own emotions in stressful situations. In these cases, our spiritual beliefs can help us achieve a perspective large enough to get some distance from our emotions and stay calm. Spiritual images such as Christ calming the raging sea can help us calm ourselves. Then we can hold our own peace better while we attend our partner's feelings and needs. Spiritual practices such as prayer, meditation, and seeking God's guidance can help us discover our calm space and look beyond our own concerns.

Another area of spiritual life that can help our relationship with our partner is being part of a community of faith: a church family. Christianity is a social religion. To quote Matthew 18:20, Christ said, "For where two or three are gathered together in my name, there am I in the midst of them." We can more easily keep our own difficulties in perspective when we have a social context in which to evaluate them. Supportive emotional connections with our faith community can help us remain in Connect Mode when stresses occur in our personal relationships.

Fixing Everything:
"Can *Love Work* solve all my relationship problems?"

You will find *Love Work* skills to be useful tools for making your relationship stable and productive. However, they are not cure-alls that automatically make everything wonderful all the time. It is important to be realistic in your expectations of each other and of your relationship. You are two different people, choosing to share your different worlds and perspectives. You will not always agree with each other. You have different emotional and physical needs. These may be in conflict at times.

The complementary differences of your personalities that attracted you to each other also mean that you will have to grow in complexity and maturity as you learn to live together with your differences. The tension you experience in this process can be frustrating at times, but a certain amount of tension also makes your lives together interesting and productive, rather than boring and lifeless.

A relationship is a life-long project. It is not something you get straight once and then forget about. It takes daily investment. Sometimes finding win/win solutions to disagreements take time. Remember that you can't necessarily resolve all your differences.

Sometimes no solution is possible, and you may just need to agree to disagree, at least for the present.

What about hurt too deep for words to reach?

Love Work shows how to use words to deal with daily hurts that, left unattended, can grow into destructive relationship obstacles. Having skills that help partners talk about daily feelings can help our lives and relationships flow smoothly.

However, sometimes bad things happen which can leave pain beyond what words can express. As a result, these deep currents may control our emotional reactions and our behavior in ways beyond our understanding. For example, a preverbal child who was often ignored by a parent may grow into an adult who feels insecure in their love relationship but has no way to talk about it.

There are feelings we or our partner may have experienced that were met with anger and rejection rather than a calm warm heart. When we get the message that certain feelings are unacceptable, we often banish those feelings from consciousness. As a result, seemingly innocuous comments or experiences may trigger painful emotional reactions and self-defeating behaviors that don't seem to make sense.

It takes courage and humility to stand calmly in the face of hurt our partner carries that cannot be described or understood. We may be tempted to babble some anxious verbal message. However, we do better when we slow down, remembering that quick words can seem unfeeling and hurtful. More than words, our partners need to know that we are there for them, even in a time of unknowing.

The holes between words can be more important than the words themselves. Hesitations let us know that our partner's mental computer is slowing down, overwhelmed by that which cannot be easily spoken. In these cases, patient silence can mean more than words. Sometimes a touch, a tear, a look of compassion, the gift of a flower are better choices to show that we care. Our calm presence in the face of the unknown, recognizing that there are some hurts that we cannot heal, will help our partner calm and mend their own unnamed wounds.

So, while *Love Work* offers ways to use words to communicate feelings, words can provide only an approximation of what goes on inside. When we recognize that words have limitations, we can use them more wisely, relying as well on nonverbal ways to build our connections with others.

Can I use *Love Work* skills with people outside of my family?

Suppose you could turn a world of frightened, grumpy, angry people into mostly friendly ones. Would you do it? You will find *Love Work* skills can improve your interactions with many people beyond your family, reducing isolation and confrontation and increasing connection, cooperation, and community.

In the work place, *Love Work* skills can help you work smoothly with peers, reduce competitive back-biting, and make the job more productive. When you are in a position of authority, using your Search Path with upset subordinates can relax them and give them space to discuss issues with you that affect their performance. Using your *Love Work* skills with your superiors is a good way to get feedback regarding your work while demonstrating your investment in the job.

Your skills can turn isolated strangers who happen to live nearby into members of your neighborhood circle of friends. You are likely to win a smile from a grumpy cashier at the grocery if you try a Search Path greeting such as, "You look tired. I imagine it has been a long day..."

Does this mean that using your Search Path or Share Path will work to help you connect with everybody? By no means. There are plenty of people out there who have no interest in having a connection with you, or even may wish to take advantage of you. In these cases, your efforts will fall on deaf ears.

However, it costs you very little to offer a human connection to others. Often, the resulting oxytocin and serotonin neurotransmitter boost you give to a stranger will be given back to you. Life is more enjoyable and meaningful when we are making each other feel good.

Notes to Myself

Notes to Myself

Notes to Myself

Chapter 11
Conclusions and Further Reading

Each Spring my wife, Polly, and I plant a garden. We protect the area from rabbits and groundhogs with a low fence. Above it we string a single strand of wire, to which we hitch an electric fence charger. We then smear peanut butter on the wire. Deer lick the wire, get shocked, and quickly learn to leave the garden area alone. This use of the Punish technique works well for deer behavioral control. Next, we amend the soil with compost and Biochar, plant tomatoes, and mulch the young plants. If we nurture and water the young plants and train them up through wire cages, we are rewarded later in the summer with delicious organic homegrown tomatoes.

Relationships work much the same way. Just as we need to protect the area in which we wish to grow tomatoes, we need to make clear boundaries in our relationships so that we know who we are taking care of and who is taking care of us. Our Share Path skills help us remain open and connected with each other and keep our relationship primary. When our partner knows what is going on with us, and we know what is going on with our partner, we will have a strong bond that nothing can break. Affairs grow, however slowly or unintentionally, in secret.

Just as soil in a garden needs to be fertilized and mulched to sustain tomato growth, relationships require nurturing as well. The Search Path skills we have been learning, through which we focus on our partner's feelings and enable our partner to focus on ours, allow us both to receive the nurture and love we need from each other. When we feel good, our energy can go into growth and development rather than into mere self-protection and survival.

Just as tomato plants need the structure of the cage to grow towards sunlight and keep their fruit off the ground, so too we need structure in our relationships in order to build habits that please our partners and to build habits in our partners that please us. The six Action Path behavioral skills we've learned enable us to provide that structure for each other.

There are myriad offenses and misunderstandings that can keep us caught up in pain and struggle with little energy left to grow and be fruitful. Most of the time, the pain and destruction that we experience goes back to how we tend our relationship garden.

If we don't have good fences, emotional entanglements from outside of the family, or interference from our extended family, the internet, smart phones, or other distractions can break into our secure space and wreak havoc.

It is important to prepare the soil of our relationship adequately. We need to take time for each other, hear each other's points of view, and also take time for ourselves. It will be more difficult to stay in Connect Mode when we haven't gotten enough exercise, eaten well, slept enough, kept a balance of work and recreation, maintained social connections, or taken time to nurture our calm peace within. When our emotional resources are exhausted, our fallback position will always be Protect Mode, with its short-term survival strategy and long-term relationship damage.

Demands of the world can eat away at the structure on which we build our lives. Just as tomatoes left on the ground tend to rot, relationships are hard to maintain when chaos reigns. Using our *LoveWork* skills can create connection and order in our lives. We can use them to make plans and build in rewards for accomplishing those plans together, rather than allowing circumstances to rule our lives. The calmer and more in control we and our partners feel, the more easily we will operate in Connect Mode, the better our decisions will be, and the more we will enjoy our lives together.

May you find peace and satisfaction with each other and hold fast to the basic deal:

I take care of you.
You take care of me.
We take care of each other.

Notes To Myself

Notes to Myself

215

Notes to Myself

216

For Further Reading

Love Work is a synthesis of psychological approaches that have contributed to our understanding of human relationships over the years. Here are some resources that can help you explore these ideas in more depth.

The Developing Mind, 2nd. ed.: How Relationships and the Brain Interact to Shape Who We Are 2015
Daniel Siegel, MD
The Guilford Press
72 Spring St.,New York, NY 10012

Hold Me Tight: Seven Conversations for a Lifetime of Love 2008
Susan M. Johnson
Little Brown and Co., Hachette Book Group
237 Park Ave. New York, NY 10017

Getting The Love You Want: A Guide for Couples 1988
Harville Hendrix
Henry Holt and Company. LLC
115 West 18th Street
New York, NY 10011

The Seven Principles for Making a Marriage Work 1999
John Gottman and Nan Silver
Three Rivers Press,
Random House, Inc.
New York, NY

Passionate Marriage: Keeping Love and Intimacy Alive in Committed Relationships 2009
David Schnarch
Henry Holt and Co. LLC
115 West 18th St. New York, NY 10011

Nonviolent Communication: A Language of Life, 3rd ed.: Life Changing Tools for Healthy Relationships 2015
Marshal Rosenberg & Deepak Chopra (Foreword)
Puddle Dancer Press
2240 Encinitas Blvd., Ste D-911,
Encinitas, CA

Full Catastrophe Living: Using the Wisdom of Your Body and Mind to Face Stress, Pain, and Illness 2005
Jon Kabat-Zinn
Bantam Dell
Random House, Inc.
New York, NY

The Relaxation and Stress Reduction Workbook, 6th ed. 2008
Martha Davis, Elizabeth Robbins Eshelman, and Matthew McKay
New Harbinger Publications, Inc
5674 Shellack Ave.
Oakland, CA 94609

Wired for Joy: A Revolutionary Method for Creating Happiness Within, 2nd. ed. 2010
Laurel Mellin, Ph.D.
Hay House Inc. NY.

Chapter 11

About the Author

Walter H. Mehring, Ed.S has been providing counseling services for individuals, couples and their families in the Charlottesville, Virginia, area for over 30 years. He earned degrees in Psychology from the College of William and Mary, and in Education and in Counseling from the University of Virginia. He has dual licensure as a Professional Counselor and as a Marriage and Family Therapist. He is skilled in family therapy, communication psychology, behavioral psychology, and brief, solution-focused methods for resolving problems of daily living.

He lives on a farm south of Charlottesville, Virginia, where he enjoys creating things that work. These include the hand-hewn log house he lives in, willow-draped ponds, bows and arrows, banjos, and a book on relationships called *Love Work*.

He is happily married to Polly, his spouse of over 45 years, and has a grown son, Jonathan. His family's struggles and triumphs over the years give him perspective in helping others with their relationships.

He is an elder at Cove Presbyterian Church.

Things I Want to Remember

Things I Want to Remember

Conclusions and Further Reading

Chapter 11